Rushing Thru the Dark

Autumn 2024
One-Act Plays, Short Screenplays, Poetry, and Art

Copyright 2024

I0559119

Choeofpleirn Press Editors
James P. Cooper, Poetry & Art
Ruth J. Heflin, Drama & Art

Choeofpleirn Press is a small, private press publishing literary journals in northeastern Kansas at the foot of the Glacial Hills. Our goal is to promote the best written and photographed creations we can in each magazine, with the eventual goal of publishing books.

Since Spring 2021, Choeofpleirn Press has published four separate journals a year: *Coneflower Café* (Spring), *Glacial Hills Review* (Summer), *Rushing Thru the Dark* (Autumn), and the *Best of Choeofpleirn Press* (Winter). The Spring, Summer, and Autumn journals are each dedicated to one of three major genres of storytelling: short fiction, nonfiction, and drama. The top three winners of the five creative contests held by CP—the Derick Burleson Poetry Prize, the Ben Nyberg Short Fiction Award, the Phil Heldrich Nonfiction Award, the Susan Hansell Drama Prize, and the Mary Cassatt Art Award—are republished in the Winter magazine. The first place award in each category comes with a cash prize.

CP also features a poem-of-the-week on our website, www.choeofpleirnpress.com.

Readers can purchase individual digital issues of each magazine directly through our website. Digital individual issues cost $6 each.

Readers who prefer print copies can purchase individual magazines from Amazon and other online bookstores.

Producers and production companies interested in performing any of the plays or screenplays should first contact the writer through the contact information in Contributors' Notes. If they do not provide a method of contacting them there, please contact Choeofpleirn Press through choeofpleirnpress@gmail.com.

Cover photo: Karen Colstrom's "Beauty Before the Storm"

ISSN (Online) 2769-0016 (Print) 2768-797X
ISBN (print) 979-8-9911790-3-4 (digital) 979-8-9911790-4-1

Editors' Note

Even though this magazine will be our last original magazine for awhile, possibly ever, there are moments of humor in the works herein.

We were told by one New York City literary entity that they would not list this magazine, *Rushing Thru the Dark*, on their database because, first, "drama is not literature," and, later, after we pointed out that it is most definitely literature, "drama has its own support...they don't need publication in literary magazines."

It was at that moment that the Coastal Elite comments my Kansas friends and relatives often derisively make hit home for me.

Of course, many large cities like NYC have support for theater, for plays and playwrights. But we exist in Kansas, where theater is almost always small production (aka "off-off-Broadway to the fourth power"), but that does not mean Kansans do not deserve to read quality plays or screenplays, and it certainly does not mean that Kansans should not publish great plays or screenplays.

Shakespeare, after all, started as a local playwright who became a national sensation.

Everyone deserves that break, that chance to reach a wider audience.

This issue brings humor in the form of a fun math problem and Krampus in *A Night Alone in Santa Fe*; in an imagined letter in, *Dear Jeff Bezos*; in a conversation between 2 males—with one clearly dominated by a narcissistic sociopath in *Best Friends;* from moments in a psychological solution to mother-in-law issues starring ancient Greek gods in *Malneirophrenia*; through an amusing look at how American family dynamics have changed over the last 60 years in *All Under One Sky*; from a comedic exploration into the importance of names in *Lost*; and in a screenplay's modern, if somewhat horrific, take on Chaucer's "Pardoner's Tale" in *The Riot Makers*.

More serious issues are also addressed, from a man's tense recounting of a moment of terror that made him remember his father in *Conflagration*, to a woman's right to say no to motherhood (and not in the way you are thinking) in *Choice*.

For an added treat is Ruth's screenplay, *Mrs. Nash,* dramatizing the life choices of the first historically documented EuroAmerican male who lived his life as a female in America.

All this and more as we rush through the dark of interstellar space in our cosmic vehicle called earth.

Choeofpleirn Press Supporters

We wish to thank the following donors for their generous support of our press:

Christine Andersen
Karyn M. Bruce
Joseph Cappello
G.W. Clift
Jeffrey Feingold
Louise Kantro
Michael Milburn
Tracy Robert
Madeline Wise

and several donors who wish to remain anonymous.

CONTENTS

ONE-ACT PLAYS

SCREENPLAYS

Alpha List of Contributors

Last Night's Monsoonal Sky

Amy Lerman

How to Summon My friendship

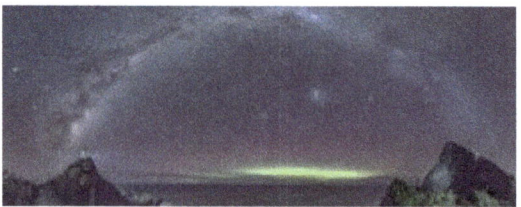

Carlee Klipsun

Tell me you're autistic too,
the variety with an ocean of empathy for
animals. Bring me a heaping pile
of abandoned kittens arranged like
wildflowers. Help me name them, but
not in a Disney princess way. Grab me a package
of blue raspberry Sour Punch Straws
from the Dollar Tree while you're there
getting cheap cat toys. Remind me to eat
a good meal between litter box trainings
because I live on cereal and almond milk. Call me
in an emergency only, like when you've found
abandoned kittens, otherwise I prefer texts. DM me
when you see a silly cat video,
and I'll do the same.

Thanksgiving Haiku

Benjamin Schmitt

1. Cranberry sauce plonks
from a can—dad laughs—time for
Thanksgiving dinner

2. Mom brings the stuffing,
looks at the setting and smiles—
shoving kids rush past

3. Kids run down the hall
laughing, screaming, playing tag—
a portrait crashes

4. Kids stand in silence,
grandpa turns from the tv,
aunt watches the game

5. Suddenly aunt screams,
the quarterback has fumbled,
then the big touchdown

6. Now all eyes are on
the replay—mom interrupts,
dinner is ready

7. Family gathered
at the table—still, no one
mentions the portrait

Peggy, Before Margaret

Andrew Graber

A Night Alone in Santa Fe

Glenn Falacienski

CHARACTERS

      MARIA, age 11, an autistic girl with too much time on her hands
      ALICIA, age 36, Maria's mother, a public school teacher on strike
      SAWYER, age 11, Maria's former friend, a nonspeaking autistic boy who died under mysterious circumstances
      THE COYOTE, age 7, Maria's friend, earnest and kind but naive about how the human world works
      FLURRIES THE ELF, indeterminate age, a bored bureaucrat who's just trying to do his job
      JOHAN, age 11, Maria's self-absorbed classmate who has a crush on her
      KRAMPUS, indeterminate age, a horned figure infamous for taking naughty children down to hell on the night of December 5

SETTING

      MARIA's house just outside of Santa Fe, New Mexico. Present day. Evening to night.

NOTES

      Dialogue that is *italicized* should be communicated in American Sign Language. A translation should be provided, with two actors representing Maria and Sawyer standing on the edge of the stage, speaking the lines. These two actors should be adults, and both should be wearing all black.

      Maria's explanation of the continuum hypothesis derives from this video: https://www.youtube.com/watch?v=UPA3bwVVzGI.

      A more advanced explanation of the hypothesis can be found here: https://www.ias.edu/ideas/2011/kennedy-continuum-hypothesis.

AT RISE

      (Soft, yellowish light on the living room and kitchen of a small house. There's an interior door in the living room and an exterior door in the kitchen. The walls are decorated with family photos and retablos.)

      (In the corner of the living room, a lit-up artificial Christmas tree sits on a towel. MARIA is taking ornaments out of a box on the floor and hanging them on the tree.)

      (An old, boxy TV is on.)

TV (NEWS)

And that's all for tonight on the Santa Fe Public Schools teachers' strike. Be sure to follow us on our Twitter page @KOB4 for updates on this story. Thank you and have a good night.

TV (COMMERCIAL)

Have you been injured in a motorcycle accident in New Mexico?

MARIA

No.

TV (COMMERCIAL)

Colton and Gutierrez will help you get the compensation that you deserve––

MARIA

> (turning off the TV)

No, they won't.

> (The phone rings. Maria sprints into the kitchen and picks up her phone off the counter.)

MARIA

Hi mom.

ALICIA (V.O.)

Hey string bean. You okay?

MARIA

Yeah.

ALICIA (V.O.)

Have you done all your homework?

MARIA

Yeah.

ALICIA (V.O.)

"Yeah," how was it? How's English going?

MARIA

Okay.

ALICIA (V.O.)

What did you do? Was it hard? Did you like it? Did you hate it?

MARIA

Well, the instructions weren't very specific, but we had to write short stories. So I wrote one about a talking coyote. It was a few pages long. It was a little hard, but not much. I didn't like it, but I also didn't hate it. I don't really know how I felt about it.

ALICIA (V.O.)

So you were ambivalent. That means that you don't really know how you feel about something. Hey, how 'bout we make that our word of the day. Can you use "ambivalent" in a sentence, Maria?

MARIA

We're still doing word of the day?

                    ALICIA (V.O.)
Education doesn't stop when school does. C'mon, give me a sentence.

        (Pause)

                    MARIA
Are you ambivalent about negotiations?

                    ALICIA (V.O.)
I––very good job. Yes, I feel ambivalent. We've come back with a new proposal, a softer one, and we've managed to get the district to talk to us. That's some progress, I suppose. But they want to cut our demands even further.

                    MARIA
So you're gonna lose?

                    ALICIA (V.O.)
I never said we'll lose. It's more likely that we'll reach a compromise.

        (Pause)

                    ALICIA (V.O.)
I know, it's disappointing. Anyway, what are you up to, since all your homework is done? What did you have for dinner?

                    MARIA
I'm putting up Christmas ornaments. And I had Cheerios and spinach. I know you like it when I eat vegetables.

                    ALICIA (V.O.)
Well, thank you. I appreciate it. Listen, baby, negotiations are gonna go pretty far into the night, so I probably won't see you until tomorrow morning. Are you going to be okay?

                    MARIA
Yeah.

                    ALICIA (V.O.)
Are you sure? If you need me, I can drive home right now. I'll find someone to take my place.

                    MARIA
I don't need you.

                    ALICIA (V.O.)
Well, if at any point you feel like you do, please give me a call.

                    MARIA
Mom, why are you so... um... why do you keep asking if I'm okay? Did I do something wrong?

                    ALICIA (V.O.)
Oh, no. I'm just stressed about the district, and I know you've been through a lot lately.

        (Pause)

MARIA

Did you know that the square root of -1 is i?

ALICIA (V.O.)

Ah, no. I didn't think that negative numbers had square roots.

MARIA

They do. The square root of -1 is i, the square root of -4 is 2i, the square root of -9 is 3i, and so on. Also, i^2 is -1, i^3 is -i, and i^4 is 1. Isn't that cool?

ALICIA (V.O.)

Spellbinding. Did you learn anything else today?

MARIA

Ummmmmmmmm... oh, I learned that tonight is Krampusnacht.

ALICIA (V.O.)

I'm sorry, tonight is what?

MARIA

Krampusnacht. It's a German holiday. That's when this big horned guy named Krampus breaks into your house, and if you've been bad he whips you with birch branches and takes you down to hell.

ALICIA (V.O.)

I see. And how exactly did you come upon this information?

MARIA

My friend Johan told me.

ALICIA (V.O.)

Johan. Is he... is he the kid who dressed up as a Christmas elf for Halloween?

MARIA

Yeah.

ALICIA (V.O.)

Okay. Maria. I know him, and I know I can't tell you who to be friends with, but, frankly, I would not encourage you to hang out with him. Johan is... rather strange.

MARIA

So am I.

ALICIA (V.O.)

You are not strange. You're special.

MARIA

What's the difference?

(Pause)

MARIA

Don't you know?

ALICIA (V.O.)

I do, baby, I do. It's just hard to explain. You're not the only one who has trouble putting things into words sometimes.

MARIA

But you're an English teacher.

ALICIA (V.O.)

That doesn't mean I'm perfect. I'm still learning too, you know.

(Pause)

ALICIA (V.O.)

So what makes you think Johan is your friend?

MARIA

He gives me strawberry Pop-Tarts sometimes. And he told me he wanted to marry me.

ALICIA (V.O.)

Sweetheart, that does not mean he's your friend. Now, he may have a little crush on you, but he's not your friend. At least not yet. Do you understand?

MARIA

No.

ALICIA (V.O.)

(sighs)

Look, baby, you're eleven now. You're not a little kid anymore. For kids your age, friendship gets to be a lot more complicated than Pop-Tarts and premature engagements.

(Pause)

ALICIA (V.O.)

I have to go now, but we can talk about this more after the strike. Okay?

MARIA

Okay.

ALICIA (V.O.)

Good night, baby.

MARIA

Please tell the district that they suck and they should be paying you a million bucks a year.

ALICIA (V.O.)

I will be sure to tell them that. See you soon.

MARIA

Bye.

(MARIA puts down the phone, then exits. She returns with an abridged *Oxford English Dictionary*, which she sets on the floor. She sits on the floor, opens the massive book, and starts leafing through the S section.)

MARIA

(Note: "spacious", "spasmodic", and "speakeasy" should all be grotesquely mispronounced.)

Spacious... spasmodic... speakeasy... special. "Having a close or exclusive connection with a specified person––"

(Power is knocked out; the entire stage goes black. We hear MARIA scream, then her footsteps as she dashes to the kitchen counter for her phone. She turns the flashlight on and sets the phone on the counter.)

(She starts walking back to the living room but decides against it and hovers in the kitchen instead.)

MARIA

Mom, where are you?

(A loud knock. MARIA runs to the exterior door. She opens it, but there's no one outside. She stands in the doorway for a few seconds, confused.)

(The knocking resumes, louder this time. It's coming from somewhere else. Maria closes the door and walks back into the kitchen, first slowly, then more quickly as she realizes where the sound is coming from.)

(She yanks open the door to the fridge. SAWYER tumbles out and engulfs her in a hug. She gives a shriek and dodges away.)

SAWYER

Sorry.

MARIA

It's okay.

Maria puts her arms around SAWYER, and he puts his arms around her. She squirms but holds the position for several seconds before they release each other.

SAWYER

Hi.

MARIA

Hi.

SAWYER

Your fridge is really cold.

MARIA

That's because it's a fridge. It's supposed to be cold.

SAWYER

I knew that. I was just trying to make small talk.

MARIA

Please don't. Small talk is boring.

SAWYER

What should we talk about, then?

MARIA

We can talk about math.

SAWYER

You always want to talk about math.

MARIA

Math is fun.

SAWYER

Math is the worst thing that ever happened to me.

MARIA

That's not true and you know it.

SAWYER

I was being sarcastic.

MARIA

Oh, shut up.

SAWYER

You shut up.

MARIA

Can we talk about what happened?

SAWYER

I was wondering when you would get to that.

MARIA

I'm getting to it right now.

SAWYER

You wanted to talk about math first.

MARIA

I'm done. I won't bring up math again. I promise.

SAWYER

They killed me.

(Pause)

MARIA

They killed you.

SAWYER

Yes.

                              MARIA
They said you drowned in the canal by yourself.

                              SAWYER
I wasn't by myself.

                              MARIA
What do you want me to do about this?

                              SAWYER
There's nothing you can do, Maria. I just wanted you to know.

                              MARIA
You're sure there's nothing I can do?

                              SAWYER
Yes.

                              MARIA
What if I tell people anyway?

                              SAWYER
Who would believe you? You're the one who gets in trouble all the time.

                              MARIA
My mom would believe me.

                              SAWYER
You need more than one person.

        (Pause)

                              MARIA
I'm sorry I left you.

                              SAWYER
Don't be sorry. It's not your fault.

                              MARIA
I can't stop thinking about it.

                              SAWYER
Me neither.

                              MARIA
What is it like where you are?

                              SAWYER
Quiet.

        (Lights flicker.)

                              SAWYER
I have to go.

MARIA

Why?

SAWYER

Ghosts can't stay in the human world for long. It makes things unstable.

(SAWYER opens a kitchen drawer. The drawer is full of strawberry Pop-Tarts. MARIA watches as he shamelessly fills his shirt with as many Pop-Tarts as he can.)

SAWYER

Thanks for these. I hope to see you again.

(Sawyer exits back through the fridge.)

(Long pause)

(MARIA stands up and tries the lights again. The power's still out.)

(She walks over to the Pop-Tart drawer and opens it.)

MARIA

Forty-three. There were fifty-two before.

(She looks up, glances from side to side.)

MARIA

Sawyer?

(She walks to the fridge and opens it. No one is inside.)

MARIA

Sawyer?

(No response.)

(MARIA goes back to the drawer and takes out a single Pop-Tart. She exits through the interior door, re-enters through the same door wearing two coats. She pulls on boots and leaves the house carrying the Pop-Tart.)

(She walks downstage and sits with her feet dangling over the edge. Shivering, she stares at the Pop-Tart.)

MARIA

Why would Johan like these so much? They look like... like... shoot, what's the word, like, uh, the food people eat when there's not a lot of food to go around––

THE COYOTE (O.S.)

Rations?

(MARIA whirls around as THE COYOTE enters and comes to sit beside her.)

MARIA

That's it. They look like rations. Like they wouldn't taste very good.

THE COYOTE

Oh no, they're great. Trust me. I found one in a garbage can the other night. It was amazeballs.

MARIA

You sure?

THE COYOTE

You know I don't lie.

(MARIA says nothing, crinkling the wrapper between her fingers.)

MARIA

Crinkly.

THE COYOTE

Aw, c'mon girl. Try it.

MARIA

I'm scared. You know how bad tastes stick in my mouth.

THE COYOTE

Hey, you know what I ate today? A rat so skinny I could see his bones through his skin. I had to bite his neck and rat blood squirted all over my face. Then I had to run back to the pups and throw up the rat so they could all get some––

MARIA
                (covering her ears)
You're not helping!

THE COYOTE

I'm just saying, however bad this tastes to you, I guarantee you half-digested rat tastes worse.

(A moment of indecision.)

THE COYOTE

Just one bite. It'll be exciting! You could use some excitement in your little human life.

MARIA

I have plenty of excitement.

(MARIA unwraps the Pop-Tart, shoves the wrapper in her pocket, and takes a teeny tiny bite. Her face contorts and she spits the food out. She sticks out her tongue and wipes it with her hand, trying to scrape off the last bits of Pop-Tart.)

THE COYOTE

Too sweet?

MARIA

Too spicy.

THE COYOTE

Spicy?

MARIA

That strawberry stuff. It burns. It's... spicy.

THE COYOTE

I can't believe this. You grew up in New Mexico and think that a Pop-Tart is spicy. You'd never survive in the wild.

MARIA

Don't remind me.

THE COYOTE

How'd you even get the Pop-Tart if you didn't wanna eat it?

MARIA

I've got a drawer full of 'em. This kid from school that I think is my friend but might not be keeps giving me these. Strawberry Pop-Tarts. I don't want to take them, but Mom said it's not polite to say no when someone offers you food. And it feels like a waste to throw them out, so I just...keep them.

THE COYOTE

You could give them to me.

MARIA

But they're not healthy.

THE COYOTE

Do I look like I care?

(Pause)

MARIA

Hey, do you think Krampus would like these?

THE COYOTE

Is Krampus the one who drags you down to hell?

MARIA

Yeah.

THE COYOTE

I thought he wasn't real. I thought you didn't believe in any of that stuff.

MARIA

I didn't. And he shouldn't be real. It's just...the ghost of my dead friend walked right out of my refrigerator, so, if ghosts are apparently real, who's to say that Krampus isn't?

(Pause)

THE COYOTE

Your dead friend came out of your refrigerator.

Right. And just before he went back into the refrigerator, he opened my Pop-Tart drawer and took nine Pop-Tarts. I know he took nine because there were fifty-two in the drawer before, and after he left there were forty-three. Apparently, Pop-Tarts are in short supply wherever he came from, and if Krampus comes from the same place, maybe he would like the Pop-Tarts, too. So my question is, do you think that if I gave Krampus all my Pop-Tarts, that would be enough to make him change his mind about sending me down to hell?

THE COYOTE

Your dead friend came out of your refrigerator.

MARIA

Did you hear my question?

THE COYOTE

Yeah, yeah, I did. I'm just having a little bit of trouble, uh, focusing on it.... What makes you think Krampus will take you to hell? I thought he only did that to bad kids.

MARIA

I haven't been a very good girl this year.

THE COYOTE

You've been good with me.

MARIA

I mean at school.

THE COYOTE

Do you, uh, wanna tell me more?

MARIA

No.

THE COYOTE

All right. Well, I'd love to camp out at your house and defend you, but I have pups to protect. 'Fraid you're on your own for this one, kid.

MARIA

You're not taking me seriously.

THE COYOTE

Yeah, I am. I know you. I know you're a good person.

(Pause)

MARIA

Do you know what the continuum hypothesis is?

THE COYOTE

Believe it or not, no, I don't.

MARIA

Okay, okay. So. You know how there's an infinity of whole numbers, right?

THE COYOTE

Right.

MARIA

And do you remember what a decimal is?

THE COYOTE

The things with the little dots.

MARIA

Basically, numbers that are between whole numbers.

THE COYOTE

Totally knew that.

MARIA

So, it makes sense that there would be an infinity of decimals, too, right?

THE COYOTE

Yeah.

MARIA

It turns out that the infinity of decimals is actually greater than the infinity of whole numbers. How is that? Well, say you had an infinite amount of time on your hands. You could, theoretically, make a list of every single whole number, right? With an infinite amount of time.

THE COYOTE

Right.

MARIA

But you couldn't make a list of all the decimals, not even if you had an infinite amount of time. Why is that? Because I'll always be able to come up with a number that's not on your list. How will I do that? I'll look at the first decimal place of the first number on your list, and I'll make my first decimal place different. Then I'll look at the second number on your list and make my second decimal place different from the second decimal place on that number. Same with the third number on your list. I'll make my third decimal place different from the third decimal place of your third number. This way, no matter how long all your decimals are, no matter how long your list is, my number won't be on it. Because my number will always have a difference of at least one digit from any number on your list. Got that?

THE COYOTE

Sure.

MARIA

Okay. So, since it's impossible to make a list of all the decimals, we can now say that the infinity of decimals is greater than the infinity of whole numbers.

THE COYOTE

So that's the continuum hypothesis.

MARIA

No no no, we're not there yet. So the infinity of decimals is greater than the infinity of whole numbers. Well, then comes the question: is it possible that there's an infinity *between* the infinity of whole numbers and the infinity of decimals? This guy called Cantor said no. And that's the continuum hypothesis.

                            THE COYOTE
Why did he say no?

                            MARIA
I don't know.

                            THE COYOTE
You don't know? I thought you were some sort of super-special math genius.

                            MARIA
I am not a super-special anything. And I'm not perfect. I won't even learn calculus until next year.

                            THE COYOTE
Oh, bummer!

                            MARIA
Yeah, it really is.

        (MARIA stands up suddenly.)

                            MARIA
I have to go.

                            THE COYOTE
Already?

                            MARIA
I have to finish putting ornaments on the Christmas tree.

                            THE COYOTE
Maria, you're gonna be fine. Krampus is not gonna take you to hell.

                            MARIA
You don't know that.

        (MARIA starts back towards her house.)

                            THE COYOTE
Maria, wait.

        (She ignores him.)

                            THE COYOTE
Maria, wait!

                            MARIA
        (turning around)
What? What is it?!

                            THE COYOTE
Can I have the rest of your Pop-Tart to take home to the pups?

MARIA

Yeah.

THE COYOTE

Thanks.

(THE COYOTE snaps up the Pop-Tart and exits.)

(MARIA goes back into her house, kicks off her boots, and throws off her two coats. She stomps over to the Christmas tree and starts hanging the ornaments with the efficiency of an assembly line worker.)

(The doorbell rings. Ornament in hand, Maria freezes in place for a second, then puts the ornament down and answers the door.)

(In the doorway stands FLURRIES THE ELF, equipped with an iPad and stylus.)

FLURRIES

(in a monotone)

Hello. My name is Flurries, and I am a magical Christmas elf. Have I reached the residence of Miss Maria?

MARIA

You're a Christmas elf—

FLURRIES

Yes.

MARIA

From the North Pole—

FLURRIES

Obviously.

MARIA

Are you sure? You're not one of those people trying to sell me something, are you?

FLURRIES

No, Miss.

MARIA

You're not one of the guys on TV who will give me money for being in a motorcycle accident?

FLURRIES

No, Miss. I assure you that I am a magical Christmas elf.

MARIA

Prove it, then. Prove that you're magical.

(FLURRIES snaps his fingers and the power comes back on.)

FLURRIES

There. Happy?

MARIA

No, that could've been a coincidence. How do I know that the power didn't just happen to come on at the exact moment that you––

(FLURRIES snaps his fingers to the tune of "Jingle Bells". Every time he snaps his fingers, the lights switch. On the final snap, the lights should come on and stay on.)

FLURRIES

Do you believe me now?

MARIA

I'm...ambivalent.

FLURRIES

Seriously?

MARIA

I mean, the probability of what you just did happening by chance is pretty much zero. But, at the same time, I just don't know how the whole Santa thing could be real.

FLURRIES

Miss, the reality of the "whole Santa thing" has been long established. Now, it appears that your residence lacks a chimney. Is there an accessible port of entry available? Is there another way to get into your house?

MARIA

Shouldn't you know that already?

FLURRIES

We're required to go around to all the houses each year to account for changes of residence.

MARIA

Then why didn't an elf come to my house last year?

FLURRIES

Miss, I hate to be rude, but I really don't have time for this. I have 1,225 more residences to visit by the end of the night. Is there an accessible port of entry available?

MARIA

Tell you what: I'll tell you how to break into my house if you answer just one question.

FLURRIES

(sighs)

Fine, but just one.

MARIA

Am I on the nice list?

FLURRIES

That's classified, Miss.

MARIA

Why?

FLURRIES

That's, uh, also classified.

MARIA

Why?

FLURRIES

All right! All right. You're on the nice list.

(Pause)

MARIA

Are you lying to me?

FLURRIES

No.

MARIA

I think you are.

FLURRIES

I most certainly am not, and I resent the accusation.

MARIA

You told me that Santa's lists were classified, but then like ten seconds later you told me I was on the nice list. That doesn't make sense. The more likely explanation—

FLURRIES

Miss, you are making things extremely difficult for me. Now if you'd just cooperate——

MARIA

I will not cooperate.

FLURRIES

If that's your choice, then Santa probably won't come see you this year.

MARIA

Okay. I'm pretty sure I'm on the naughty list anyway.

FLURRIES

All right, then. I'll mark you down as noncompliant. Let's see here...

(FLURRIES taps and swipes at the iPad with the stylus. His face scrunches up. He jabs at the iPad with perhaps more force than necessary.)

(under his breath)

Son of a poinsettia.

MARIA

What's wrong?

                    FLURRIES
Oh, Apple did some kinda update last night, and now I can't figure out how to work the thing.

                    MARIA
Maybe I could fix it.

                    FLURRIES
That won't be necessary.

                    MARIA
You sure? I'm good with computers.

                    FLURRIES
Oh, all right.

        (FLURRIES hands MARIA the iPad. She solves the problem immediately and hands it
        back to him.)

                    FLURRIES
Impressive.

                    MARIA
Thank you.

        (The phone rings.)

                    MARIA
Merry Christmas.

        (MARIA closes the door and rushes to pick up the phone.)

                    MARIA
Who is this?

                    JOHAN (V.O.)
Maria? It's me, Johan.

                    MARIA
Oh. Hi.

                    JOHAN (V.O.)
Hey, um, so––sorry this is awkward, but, um, I was wondering if, uh, maybe you wanted to go
to the lighting ceremony with me?

                    MARIA
The lighting ceremony on the plaza?

                    JOHAN (V.O.)
Yeah. Um, it's this Saturday at six. Are you free?

                    MARIA
My mom says that's for tourists.

JOHAN (V.O.)
My mom says the whole city's for tourists.

MARIA
I know. It's so expensive we can't afford to live there anymore. That's why we had to move out here.

JOHAN (V.O.)
Tell me about it! And they raised gas prices by ten cents. What is this state coming to?

MARIA
I don't know.

JOHAN (V.O.)
Me neither. I was just being random.

MARIA
I can tell.

JOHAN (V.O.)
I'm so weird sometimes.

MARIA
Me, too.

JOHAN (V.O.)
Isn't it hard being surrounded by normies all day?

MARIA
You know what? Yes! Yes, it is.

JOHAN (V.O.)
What do they even think about?

MARIA
I have no idea.

JOHAN (V.O.)
Their heads are so...empty. So stagnant.

MARIA
And all they do is talk! Every chance they get. It's like if they stopped talking they'd just...explode or something.

JOHAN (V.O.)
Ugh, Maria, I feel you so hard. I feel like you just get me, you know?

	(Pause)

MARIA
That's the first time anyone has ever said that to me.

JOHAN (V.O.)
Well, you deserve to hear it.

(Pause)

JOHAN (V.O.)

So, are you free on Saturday?

MARIA

Johan, can I ask you something?

JOHAN (V.O.)

Of course.

MARIA

Are you autistic?

JOHAN (V.O.)

What?

MARIA

I said are you——

JOHAN (V.O.)

Why would you think that?

MARIA

Well...you were talking about how weird you are, and I have autism, and we seem to be connecting——

JOHAN (V.O.)

You have autism?

MARIA

Yeah.

JOHAN (V.O.)

No way. You don't look autistic.

MARIA

Wha——why not?

JOHAN (V.O.)

You're pretty and smart and...kind of a badass, for real. There's no way you could be autistic.

MARIA

But I am.

JOHAN (V.O.)

No, you aren't. Believe me, I know an unfortunate amount about this subject. I have a cousin on the spectrum, and he's nothing like you.

MARIA

I have a cousin who's normal, and he's nothing like you.

JOHAN (V.O.)

I'm sorry, did you just call me normal?

MARIA

Yes.

JOHAN (V.O.)

I am not normal. I'm weird. I don't know what it is, but I just don't fit in.

MARIA

Okay.

JOHAN (V.O.)

And so are you! You're weird like me. You're not autistic.

MARIA

Yes, I am.

JOHAN (V.O.)

Maria, I'm telling you. Autistic people are like that kid who wandered off and drowned in the canal. They have, like, no sense of reality, okay? That's not you.

(Long pause.)

MARIA

Don't ever talk to me again.

JOHAN (V.O.)

What? What did I say?

MARIA

I said, don't ever talk to me again. Not at school. Not on the phone. Never. Ever. Again. Got it?

JOHAN (V.O.)

Maria——

(MARIA hangs up. She walks back to the Christmas tree and resumes hanging the ornaments, more slowly this time.)

(The exterior door swings open. In the doorway is KRAMPUS.)

(KRAMPUS creeps towards MARIA. She appears to be oblivious to him——until she turns around, grabs the dictionary off the floor, and hurls it at him with all of her strength.)

(The dictionary misses KRAMPUS by a solid five feet.)

KRAMPUS

That was a terrible throw.

MARIA

Are you gonna take me to hell?

KRAMPUS

I don't take kids to hell. I eat them alive.

MARIA

Are you gonna eat me alive, then?

KRAMPUS

No. Listen, could I get some of your chocolate soy milk? It's been a day.

MARIA

Um, sure.

(KRAMPUS opens the fridge and takes out the chocolate soy milk. He retrieves a glass—somehow he knows exactly where the glasses are—from the cupboard, then turns to MARIA.)

KRAMPUS

Do you want some too?

MARIA

Yeah.

(KRAMPUS fills two glasses with chocolate soy milk. He sits down at the kitchen table and motions for MARIA to join him.)

KRAMPUS

Well, come on, then. Don't just stand there.

MARIA

But I don't wanna get eaten.

KRAMPUS

I'm not going to eat you.

MARIA

How do I know you're not lying?

KRAMPUS

Maria, right now, I just want to have some milk, and I hate having milk by myself. Please. Sit down.

(So she sits down across from him. They both guzzle their milk.)

KRAMPUS

That hit the spot. Want some more?

MARIA

Could we not have more milk, actually?

KRAMPUS

What do you mean?

MARIA

Well, my mom's on strike right now, which means she hasn't been paid in a week, and soy milk is way more expensive than dairy milk, but I need it because I'm lactose intolerant––

                          KRAMPUS
Oh, I'm so sorry. No more milk then.

                          MARIA
Are you gonna eat me now?

                          KRAMPUS
No.

                          MARIA
Why not?

                          KRAMPUS
Do you want me to eat you?

                          MARIA
No. But you only eat bad kids, right?

                          KRAMPUS
Yes.

                          MARIA
And I've been bad. I can prove it. I can remember every single bad thing I've done this year.

                          KRAMPUS
Can you really.

                          MARIA
On January 10th, Ella was making fun of me 'cause I said the word "ballet" wrong. I thought it was pronounced like "ballot." She kept saying, "I can't believe you didn't know!" So I told her to shut the Sam Hill up, and I got in a lot of trouble for that.

                          KRAMPUS
Hm.

                          MARIA
And then on January 15th, Mom and I were driving to Gallup to see my cousins. Well, I wasn't driving. Mom was. Anyway, I kept singing the "Unit Circle Song" over and over again because I liked the sound of it so much, and Mom yelled at me.

And then, on January 16th, I was at my cousins' house playing with my Legos, and my aunt Piper was trying to ask me if I'd gotten my period yet, and I said no, but then she started screaming her head off because I didn't look up at her when I said no.

                          KRAMPUS
What a shame.

                          MARIA
And then, on January 22nd, I got in a lot of trouble because I moved my hands. I was in English class, and it was really hard, with all the words, so I was moving my hands. And the teacher was like, "You need to have quiet hands," but I couldn't because I just needed to move my hands, you know? She got so mad at me she called my mom. And then my mom was like, "Why can't you just keep your hands under your desk?"

                              KRAMPUS
Are we done yet?

                               MARIA
No.

                              KRAMPUS
How many more of these incidents do you have to go?

                               MARIA
Twenty-two.

                              KRAMPUS
In the interest of saving time, could you just pick the worst one?

                               MARIA
But they were all bad.

                              KRAMPUS
Surely one or two stick out.

                               MARIA
Stick out of what?

                              KRAMPUS
It's an expression. I mean, surely one or two are worse than the others.

    (Pause)

                               MARIA
On November 16th, I was at my friend Sawyer's house, and I left because I had a lot of math homework to do. I left him home alone.

                              KRAMPUS
That doesn't sound so bad.

                               MARIA
And then his parents came home and killed him.

                              KRAMPUS
Oh...okay. Um. I wasn't expecting that.

                               MARIA
I wasn't either.

                              KRAMPUS
How do you know his parents killed him?

                               MARIA
His ghost told me.
                              KRAMPUS
So nobody else knows?

MARIA

I don't think so. They made it look like an accident. They told everybody he wandered away and drowned in the canal.

KRAMPUS

I'm failing to see how this is your fault. You didn't know they would kill him.

MARIA

I knew other things, though.

KRAMPUS

Other things?

MARIA

He was autistic. Like me. And his parents didn't want that. They wanted a normal kid. They were trying to treat him with all sorts of garbage. Pills and stuff. I think they gave him cleaning fluid once. They tried to make him act normal, so that he could blend in. When he didn't, they wouldn't feed him. Sometimes, they wouldn't let him drink water.

KRAMPUS

Did you tell anyone about it?

MARIA

I told my mom. I told a couple other people, but they didn't believe me.

(Pause)

MARIA

Is that enough to make you change your mind about eating me?

KRAMPUS

No.

MARIA

Not even a little?

KRAMPUS

I knew I wasn't going to eat you before I even walked in the door.

MARIA

But how did you know?

KRAMPUS

I just did.

MARIA

Is that how Santa knows who's on the naughty list?

KRAMPUS

No, Santa has an international surveillance system. I just wing it.

MARIA

Then why did you come to my house?

                                KRAMPUS
Because I wanted some chocolate soy milk. But now, I also want to show you something.

        (KRAMPUS stands up and walks to the fridge.)

                                KRAMPUS
Follow me.

        (KRAMPUs exits through the fridge.)

        (MARIA hesitates, then runs to the fridge and exits as well.)

        (House lights come up just enough for the audience to see each other and the aisles.
        MARIA and KRAMPUS enter through the back of the house and walk through the aisle.)

                                KRAMPUS
Stay close to me now. I've never taken a human down here before, and I want to make sure I
can get you back up.

                                MARIA
Who are these people?

                                KRAMPUS
Ghosts. Just like your friend. Maria, I don't know if you're religious, but I'm getting the sense
that you aren't——

                                MARIA
I'm not.

                                KRAMPUS
——but there's no heaven or hell. Only this. We call it the in-between.

                                MARIA
And why exactly are we here?

                                KRAMPUS
Maria, are you familiar with the continuum hypothesis?

                                MARIA
Of course. The continuum hypothesis is the idea that there's nothing between the infinity of
whole numbers and the infinity of decimals.

        (Pause. KRAMPUS looks away from MARIA.)

                                MARIA
Isn't that right?

                                KRAMPUS
It's close enough, I suppose.

                                MARIA
Close enough?! What's that supposed to mean?

KRAMPUS

The true continuum hypothesis states, "There is no set whose cardinality is strictly between that of the integers and the real numbers." An integer is, as you said, a whole number. A real number is essentially any number that can be found on a number line, both rational and irrational. I assume you understand the difference between rationals and irrationals, yes?

MARIA

Yes, I do.

KRAMPUS

Good. Now the continuum hypothesis has been contested throughout history. It was the first of Hilbert's problems. Gödel constructed a model of set theory that proved the hypothesis right, and Cohen constructed a model of set theory that proved the hypothesis wrong. So, basically, both men used simplified ways of looking at the world to fit their own ideas about the hypothesis.

MARIA

So it hasn't been solved.

KRAMPUS

No, it hasn't. We can't say that it's right, and we can't say that it's wrong. Many people have tried to put it in one category or the other, and I'm sure that in the future they'll be thinking about it still. But we may never have a definite answer.

MARIA

That's disappointing.

KRAMPUS

I suppose. Anyway, the point that I'm trying to make here is that... well, remember how I said there's no heaven or hell?

MARIA

Yeah.

KRAMPUS

And yet billions of people want to believe that when they die they'll go to either heaven or hell, the same way that mathematicians want to believe that the continuum hypothesis is either right or wrong. You humans always want to put things into categories. I don't know why, but you do. But that's just not how the world works.

MARIA

The continuum hypothesis is neither true nor false.

KRAMPUS

Correct. And most people don't go to heaven or hell. They end up here, in the in-between.

MARIA

Most people?

KRAMPUS

Well, I do end up eating a few of them. But the vast majority go here. Your friend went here. And one day you'll go here. You're not a bad person. I don't mean to say that you're a good person, either. You're just——you're rather ordinary, to be honest.

MARIA

I'm ordinary.

KRAMPUS

Does that offend you?

MARIA

A little.

KRAMPUS

You'll get over it.

(The house lights flicker.)

KRAMPUS

Our time grows short.

MARIA

What's wrong?

KRAMPUS

I don't bring humans down here and this is why. It makes things unstable.

MARIA

Then we've got to go back.

(MARIA makes towards the back of the house, but KRAMPUS stops her.)

KRAMPUS

Not that way. Unless you want all these ghosts bursting through your fridge. Follow me again.

(KRAMPUS runs to the edge of the stage and hoists himself up. The house lights dim.)

KRAMPUS

C'mon, quickly!

(MARIA climbs up onto the stage as both the house and stage lights go dark. When the stage lights go up again, KRAMPUS is gone. MARIA finds herself just outside her house.)

(She runs into her house and opens the fridge. Nothing out of the ordinary.)

(She runs outside, to the spot where she came back from the in-between. She stares out at the audience but sees nothing.)

(She runs back inside and checks the Pop-Tart drawer. It's empty.)

(She exits through the interior door, comes back with a piece of paper and a pencil. She sits down on the floor and, using the dictionary to support the paper, starts writing a note.)

MARIA

(to herself)

Mom, there is something I need to tell you about Sawyer...

(The phone rings. MARIA jumps up and grabs it.)

MARIA

Mom?

ALICIA (V.O.)

Hey baby. Good news: the strike is over. We got most of our demands met.

MARIA

Most of them?

ALICIA (V.O.)

Well, I never thought we'd get all of them. But things could've been a lot worse. Every single one of us gets a five percent raise. I know, it's great. Listen, I am exhausted, so I will see you later. Have you gotten ready for bed yet?

MARIA

No.

ALICIA (V.O.)

Not at all?

MARIA

No.

ALICIA (V.O.)

Sweetheart, it's after midnight. What have you been doing all this time?

(Long pause.)

ALICIA (V.O.)

That sounds like an illustrious night, but you have school tomorrow. You excited to be back in school?

MARIA

No.

ALICIA (V.O.)

Well, regardless, I want you in bed by the time I get home. Okay?

MARIA

How long will it take you to get home?

ALICIA (V.O.)

I am not going to tell you that because I know that if I do, you'll wait until I'm a foot away from the door to put your pajamas on. Consider your timer starting now. See you soon.

MARIA

Bye, Mom.

(MARIA goes to the Christmas tree, which she still hasn't finished decorating. She rummages around in the ornament box until she finds the star. She stands tip-toed on the couch and stretches to place the star on top of the tree. Then she turns off the tree lights.)

(She stops for a second and stares in the direction of the audience, though she still can't see them.)

MARIA

Good night, everybody.

(She walks through the house, turning off the rest of the lights. Finally, she exits.)

END OF PLAY.

There's Something Ancient Here

McKenna Wilds

We give Dog a new toy
and she skins the tennis ball

or smiling fox or floppy bird
and there's something uncomfortable

and ancient about it all.
Our sweet, fluffy Dog

inherited a touch of violence
from her ancestors. Camouflaged

and accepted now, because
it's cute? Here she is

excited about the squeaker
she found. Squeak. Squeak!

Squeeeeeeaaak! With every bite,
the sound of a dying animal

crying. What fun
in a neon green Target toy!

No more squeaker toys,
I say. Bones instead.

Like the scraps humans gave wolves
that created dogs thousands of years ago.

Instead, I toss a toy rope in front of Dog
with an optimistic smile.

Ropes: no sound, no spine, no history.
Dog looks at it then at me then goes to sleep.

Central Europe #3f

Kenneth Kesner

Nightwalking

Frank William Finney

Tears crawl
like spiders—

webs for the face.

A dreary walk
in a dreary town—

Nobody else near
to see or hear

the circling bats;
the owls in my head.

And yet there's solace
in the streetlights' haze—

And mine
the only footfall.

DEAR JEFF BEZOS

Excerpt from the two-act play, *Letters to Jeff Bezos*

Susan Hansell

SYNOPSIS
   A Hot Guy addresses his thoughts to Jeff Bezos.

CHARACTERS
   THE HOT GUY (basically good-natured; a male-identified actor of any age or
   ethnicity)

SET AND TECH
   A writing table or a writing desk that faces the audience, or simply a chair or a
   stool.

PROPS
   A small laptop or paper and pen. THE HOT GUY might write on a small
   electronic device or with paper and pen or he may choose not to write at all,
   whichever the director and the performer choose.

TEXTUAL NOTE
   Dropped down line separations within individual characters' lines are meant to
   approximate breaks in flow for breathing and reflection that are shorter than the
   silences noted in orchestrated beats and pauses, though ultimately such timing
   choices are up to the performers and their direction.

FADE UP TO:
   THE HOT GUY sits at a table or at a desk, or on a chair or stool, with either a
   small electronic device or with paper and pen or with nothing at all.

   A brief pause at the start will allow the audience to absorb the minimal scene.

   THE HOT GUY will address Jeff Bezos as if he is "everywhere" or "in the air" or
   "there" (as in the audience).

   At the same time, THE HOT GUY is writing and speaking to himself, and
   basically knows it, and enjoys entertaining and musing over his own thoughts.

Jeff!

I saw you at Coachella. With like, fifty bodyguards.

    (beat)

Be awesome, dude. Lose the bodyguards.

    (pause)

Did your new GF talk you into Coachella, Jeff? Or were you trying to impress her with your youthful exuberance?

I kid, I kid.

    (beat)

Any prenup on that thing must be something. I can picture it.

No, I can't.

    (beat)

Maybe you'll opt out of the marriage thing. Protect the assets. The brand.

What's next, Jeff? Burning Man?

I've been there. In a good way. Natch.

    (thoughtfully)

You and me, we're not getting any younger, are we Jeff?

It's gotta be hard wondering if people like you, for you.

    (beat)

I'm only a middle school teacher, yet I know my girlfriend likes me for me.

It's definitely not a money thing.

It's not a this-guy-is-a-weirdo-but-he's-the-richest-man-in-the-world thing.

    (THE HOT GUY takes visual tock of himself.)

You know?

    (beat)

The problem I have, Jeff, is that I don't resist.

People come up to me. I don't resist.

Is that the same as *choosing*? As *liking*?

I mean, did *I* choose? Or did I *go along*?

(sighs)

I dunno dude.

I'm not sure I ever choose. Chose. Anything.

(shrugs)

Thus, the ambivalence.

(beat)

I'm not saying I'm a jerk. I'm not a jerk. OK perhaps a bit of a jerk. At times. I've been told.

Aren't we all?

(beat)

Don't judge me, Jeff.

(pause)

I remember once — being chosen and choosing at the same time. Which is, I suppose, like falling for someone at the same time they fall for you. Which is nice. It was nice.

But I blew it.

(beat)

Whatever that means. Whatever I meant by that. Whatever I mean now.

Because honestly, Jeff. I do not know.

(pause)

I think about this simultaneous falling, the choosing.

Those days, spending that time — because you do spend it — time — ... it seemed... flawless.

(beat)

I remember...

Not One. Cracked. Plate.

(aside)

Unexpected metaphor, I know.

(aside off)

But if that's true, and it can't be true, because there's no such thing as flawlessness, then what I'm dealing with, what I'm feeling, is nostalgia. Simple nostalgia, Jeff. And nostalgia isn't real.

(sighs)

Feelings are tough, Jeff.

(pause)

I don't want to be alone.

(beat)

At the same time, not wanting to be alone makes things...
Involved.

(beat)

Doesn't it?

(suddenly up beat)

Maybe that's your problem too!

(surprised grin)

Jeff! What I want to know is — with your money and your space flights and with possibly wife 2.0 — *do you know how you feel*?

(long pause)

Hey have you heard of that incel theory?

Those angry guys who believe 5% of the men get 90% of the relationships?

I'm not sure about the math on that or if it's factual. It probably isn't factual. It's probably a way for them to get mad.

Regardless. You and me Jeff, we don't have to worry.

    (THE HOT GUY takes visual stock of himself again.)

I mean, me.

    (beat)

We know what *you have*.

Not to say that you didn't have looks to begin with. You might've. Youth in itself is a beautiful thing.

But whether you did or you didn't, the reality is, today, you have to wonder, don't you?

That's different from me.

At least, I think it's different.

    (considers)

I don't count on anything expensive, this much is certain.

Yet we all age.

Which isn't necessarily a problem.

Not that I don't think about it.

    (thinks)

I do. I do think about it.

Because then what? Then what happens?

    (beat)

I think you know, Jeff...

    (suddenly upbeat again)

Which is why I want to pick your brain!

    (THE HOT GUY laughs until his laughter trails off into uncertainty.)

Yeah... . Money lasts. If you're careful. Looks, not so much.

We went over that.

And feelings.

How can you know?

    (sighs)

Which means you're a lucky guy, Jeff.

I think.

    (beat)

We both are.

    (with a thumbs-up)

Have fun up there, dude.

    (to himself or to the audience)

That's what's up.

    (THE HOT GUY might make a thumbs-up or the ASL "I love you" hand sign or one of his own choice.

    (Beat.)

    (Slow fade out.)

END.

Reconsider

Megan Munger

As the sun sets at 9:33 PM on June 26th, I ask it
to reconsider. I glance into black bushes
and remain silent, a predator, as the sky turns

Cabernet. Reconsider because I'm not yet done
with today. I've spend it here on this patio
reading, writing in baby blue pen, trying
to enjoy being broke down a dirt road,

unprepared for everything. I need more time
on one of the longest days of the year,
how outrageous am I, but darkness isn't
the same out here without streetlights.

The only sound is the cows as they move
into their barn for the night. Darkness isn't
a shroud to clothe my flaws like it used to be.

When we met at the college park, my high school
boyfriend asked me, *have you ever reconsidered?*
All he wanted was for me to come back, to be his girl.

Unlike when we were sixteen, he had money,
time, a better understanding, more
maturity. He made it sound easy—why
can't I just leave, go be with him in the city?
With our new cars, graduations soon,

it would be perfect timing, accomplished
like we always promised. When I got up
to leave, it felt like it does out here tonight. Wrong

and why did I come here? I want
to go home. I need to go apologize
for the pain I've caused, reconsider
my safety in the arms of a man I met
ten days after we broke up. I've loved him

and stayed here ever since. Reconsider how
the night sky makes me feel like Macbeth's wife.
Reconsider how I turn the key to lock us in.

Bee Hawk Moth

Karen Colstrom

The March for No Reason

Stephen Philip Druce

"Let's do a march for no reason" muttered Stevie in one of his drunken epiphanies. "A what?" retorted Louis looking bewildered. "A march for no reason, it's never been done. If we don't make it as musicians we'll never be remembered" said Stevie enthusiastically. Stevie had always been obsessed with fame. Blighted by anxiety and a booze addiction however, his dreams of becoming a rock star were unfulfilled. The march for no reason was an opportunity for him to leave his mark as the founder of the world's first march for no reason - "it's genius" said Louis.

The town's statue was the appointed location for the march and posters were printed off to promote the event. Louis girlfriend Sarah looked pensive - "Louis I'm worried. What if the march is sabotaged by anarchists?. It may turn violent, we could be arrested for orchestrating an illegal gathering, can't you cancel it?". "I'm worried too" said Louis, "but we've come too far to turn back now. This is Stevie's last chance to leave a significant legacy. He'll never make it in music industry now".

On September 4th 1993, Stevie, Louis and Sarah made their way to the statue, anticipating hundreds in attendance but the turn out was just forty two. The police arrived in large numbers and the senior officer approached Louis as he was positioned at the front of the group. "What's all this about then?" asked the officer sternly. "It's not about anything" replied Louis - Sarah giggled. "Well you need permission for an organised protest" said the officer.

On cue as planned, Stevie stood up and
yelled "come on marchers, let's go to
the park!". Stevie's cunning plan had
been executed to perfection. He'd foreseen
that should the police enforce a crowd
dispersal, it would subsequently prompt
a unified movement of the marchers that
would naturally walk away in the same
direction. The proposed destination for
the march was predetermined too, and
Stevie knew the police would have to
follow them, giving the protest the desired
credibility. A lengthy line of officers had
cordoned off the gates at the park entrance.
As Stevie was leader he felt his duty was
to climb the gates in a show of defiance,
but was apprehended. The marchers burst
into their adopted anthem song for the day -
"all we are saying, is nothing at all!".
Louis pulled Stevie back from the skirmishes -
"Stevie get back you're drunk, you'll get
arrested. Photographs have been taken,
we've got proof, you've made history!".

BEST FRIENDS

A play in one act
Michael Riordan

CHARACTERS
    DAVE—A bespectacled man, who is nervous and insecure
    JOHN—Dave's Friend, who is confident and self-assured

SETTING
    Blinky's restaurant-bar.

TIME
    Evening/after work.

AT RISE
    (DAVE is sitting at a small table, waiting for his friend John to arrive. A large bottle, two tall glasses of beer, and a small cardboard tray of french fries are on the table. When JOHN enters, he looks around before spotting DAVE, who is immediately relieved.)

DAVE

Hey John, over here!
    (The two friends greet; Dave offers John a seat.)

JOHN

Dave, how are you? Sorry--I checked my messages after work and saw yours. I came as soon as I could.

DAVE

I know, John, and--hey-- thanks for being here, man. Hope I didn't keep you from anything.

JOHN

Hey, Dave, we're friends. A friend sends out an SOS, needs help, I go. That's the way I am.

DAVE

I know John, and I really appreciate it. Anyway, here, this is for you.

(DAVE pushes a glass of beer towards JOHN. JOHN will munch on the fries throughout DAVE's urgent pleas for help.)

I got you a drink and a snack—French fries.

JOHN

Thanks, man.

>   (JOHN takes a sip and his mouth expresses displeasure, then shoves a few fries in his mouth.)

DAVE

John, the reason I asked you here—

JOHN

>   (Still chewing)

Dave, it's warm. Warm beer, Dave.

DAVE

What's that, John?

JOHN

Never mind, Dave. So what were you saying?

DAVE

Yeah. So, what I was saying is that—you and I are friends, right?

JOHN

Dave...David...the very question offends me. Of course we're friends. A friend sends out an SOS, needs help, I go. (emphasizes each word) It's-the-way-I-am.

DAVE

And you don't know how much that means to me, John. Really. You know, John, when I moved to this city over ten years ago, you were good enough to, well, show me around, introduce me to the gang at work—you really made me feel welcome.

JOHN

Of course, Dave—and I'd do it all again. You know that. Hey, remember that first night—right here at Blinky's Bar with the guys—and you drank too much and got violently sick?

DAVE

Yeah. I got sick all over a policeman, John. But the reason I—

JOHN

--That's right. You threw up on a cop who threatened to arrest you and throw you in jail. But we guys talked him out of it, explained that you were from out of state, just moved here, new to the area and all that. The cop—he understood and was good humored about the whole thing.

DAVE

John, he made me eat my driver's license.

JOHN

You're lucky it wasn't your vehicle registration, Dave.

DAVE

Yeah. I guess so. I suppose it could have been worse. But you were there for me that night.

JOHN

That's what friendship is all about, Dave. (Squeezing a pack of ketchup onto his fries and looking around) You know, it wouldn't hurt if they gave you a couple of extra packets of ketchup. But forget it. Go on.

DAVE

Right, John. I just needed to talk to you. You know, I remember later that first year. We were sitting down together at a place like this. You turned to me and said, "Dave, you are my best friend." I was moved. I was touched—

JOHN

--We met in 2012, right? (He's thinking carefully.)

DAVE

Right. 2012, and you said I was your best friend.

JOHN

No. I don't think so, Dave.

DAVE

Yes. You told me that first year that I was your best friend. And I was moved, I was touched—

JOHN

--Now wait, Dave, what time of the year was it?

DAVE

Well, I don't know. Does it make a difference?

JOHN

Because, you see, Frank Hennessy was my best friend in 2012.

DAVE

Frank Hennessy?

JOHN

Yeah. I'm sure of it. But you're my best friend now. That's what counts—and I'm here to help.

DAVE

Frank Hennessy cheats at cards.

JOHN

Frank Hennessy also cheats at darts, golf, and on his wife. But in 2012 Frank Hennessy was my best friend. What can I say?

DAVE

All right. Sorry, John. Anyway, I knew I could count on you tonight.

JOHN

Absolutely. So, what is it?

DAVE

Well, John, I've always felt that, well, that you and I were on the same wavelength, that we connected--and when one of my signals flashed out, then your antenna would receive.

JOHN

(Distracted) What are you trying to say, Dave. Anything left in that bottle?

DAVE

Yeah, sure. (pours drink) What I was saying is, well, I've always thought that you really know what I am all about, that you see me, that you know where I am coming from—I mean, as a, uh, human being on this planet.

JOHN

Oh. As a human being—

DAVE

--on this planet.

JOHN

Right. I hear you now. What you're in fact talking about is really the affinity between two human beings—that is, the inter-human connection—which of course is the essence of friendship.

DAVE

That's it exactly, John.

JOHN

What I'm getting here, what I see here before me, is the picture of a guy who is crying out for help. Your face might as well have "HELP" written all over it.

DAVE

Yes, that's the word: "Help."

JOHN

Capital 'H' in red.

DAVE

Exactly. Red. Blood red. I'm bleeding, John.

JOHN

I hear you, Dave.

DAVE

I knew you would, John.

JOHN

So. (Pounds table with both hands) Dump everything you have right here. Rip your guts open.

DAVE

(Removes calendar from his bag or briefcase. He tosses calendar on the table.)

JOHN

What's this, Dave? Is this a wall calendar? So—

DAVE

--2024, John. This whole past year—Disaster. My Titanic year! There are hundreds of squares on this calendar, John. See, I've written "Disaster' on each one.

                                   JOHN
Yeah. You've also drawn little icebergs in the corner of each little square. Effective—

                                   DAVE
--But, John, I'm telling you, it really has been awful.

                                   JOHN
You've had a few bad breaks over the year. That's all. But 2024 is almost gone, Dave. There's a new year on the horizon. Forget this Titanic business, Dave. Launch a new ship.

                                   DAVE
I don't know if I can do that, John.

                                   JOHN
Of course, you can.

                                   DAVE
My boat is sunk, John.

                                   JOHN
Nonsense, Dave. The key is the big 'P'.

                                   DAVE
The big 'P'?

                                   JOHN
The big 'P' Dave. Perspective. You're looking at life all wrong. You're missing some of life's messages, some of its signals.

                                   DAVE
I am?

                                   JOHN
Of course. You need to look at life differently. You need to look directly at life, grab it with both hands, and take control.

                                   DAVE
But I've tried so hard. (pause) Look at this, John. (He reaches into his bag.) I've read every self-help book in print.

                                   JOHN
What have you got here? "Love is Letting Go of Fear."

                                   DAVE
John, I wish you wouldn't—

                                   JOHN
--War is Letting Go of Peace."

                                   DAVE
John, really—

                                   JOHN
"Vegetarianism is Letting Go of Meat."

                           DAVE

You see, John?

                           JOHN

What I see is a person who doesn't know <u>how</u> to see. (Removing Dave's glasses) Let me have your glasses, Dave.

                           DAVE

But I need them—

                           JOHN

--No, you don't. I'm your eyes now, Dave, and I'm going to show you how wrong you've been.

                           DAVE

(Squinting, groping) You're going to have to show me where my car is, too, John—I really can't see a thing without those glasses.

                           JOHN

Will you forget about the glasses, Dave. You're missing the point. Now what's the worst thing that happened to you during the year? That thing in Tibet—with your grandparents slipping off the mountain during the avalanche? Is that what's upsetting you?

                           DAVE

Well, yeah, that was bad enough—but they were old, John. They've climbed their mountains. No, I'm not talking about that, but it <u>was</u> something I lost.

                           JOHN

Something you lost?

                           DAVE

Lost, John. It was—

                           JOHN

--Don't tell me, Dave. Let me guess. Your first edition of Ernest Hemingway's <u>Old Man</u> <u>and the</u> <u>Sea.</u> It's just a fish story, Dave.

                           DAVE

No, John—

                           JOHN

Hey, you didn't lose that souvenir I brought back to you from my Europe trip—the leaning tower of Pisa combination thermometer and sunscreen dispenser?

                           DAVE

No, it's still there on the mantel next to the framed photograph of my grandparents before their Tibet trip—I <u>told</u> Grandma to get some new hiking boots—No, John, what I lost is something inside me. I don't know what it is, but one day I woke up...and that something was gone. It's hard to describe it, but it was gone. I looked for it, John. I've been on my hands and knees all year. And I still haven't found it. I mean, do you understand?

                           JOHN

Believe me, Dave. I've tried to understand you. I've studied you from a distance, and I've studied you up close—and to me you're still a—

DAVE

You're not going to call me an 'enigma', are you, John? I hate the actual <u>word</u> more than I hate being one.

JOHN

No, Dave. Because I think I understand you at last. A friend sends up a flare—a distress signal--I answer it. I chip away at the problem until I find the solution. You say you've tried everything?

DAVE

But I have. I mean...the books—

JOHN

Perspective, Dave. The big 'P'. Now look, Dave. (Takes the beer bottle in his hand.) Take a look at this, Dave. What do you see?

DAVE

An empty beer bottle.

JOHN

Of course. That's what <u>you</u> see. Ask me what <u>I</u> see, Dave.

DAVE

What do you see, John?

JOHN

I see potential, Dave.

DAVE

Potential?

JOHN

Potential.

DAVE

Is that a little 'p' or a big 'P'?

JOHN

Potential, Dave. This bottle <u>will</u> be filled again. This bottle will be recycled and filled again.

DAVE

You want me to be recycled, John?

JOHN

What I want, Dave, is for you to open your eyes and to begin to see things that are not there.

DAVE

You want me to see things that are not there.

JOHN

Exactly. Now we'll try again with this little box of wooden matches. I'll slide it open—now just pick a matchstick, Dave. (DAVE does so.) What have you got?

DAVE

A match.

JOHN

Look again, Dave.

DAVE

Well, it's a burnt match. The match has been used and stuck back in the box.

JOHN

Ah Hah!

DAVE

I chose the burnt match.

JOHN

Which tells you?

DAVE

Burnt. Flame gone...uh...blackness. Used. Discarded.

JOHN

Good!

DAVE

You're right, John.

JOHN

Of course, I am. Now watch. (grabs matchbox.) I choose. Behold. My match is fresh, new, full of potential life and bright flame, the potential to light the world and set it on fire.

DAVE

Oh yes, John. I see it. And you could do it, too.

JOHN

Here, Dave. Catch.

(John tosses a bottle top to Dave)

DAVE

Bottle top...ah...beer bottle top. Got it. (pause) What should I do with it, John?

JOHN

Well, flip it of course, like a coin.

DAVE

(Catches bottle top in the air)

Okay. Right.

JOHN

Well?

                                DAVE
You're right again, John. It's me. I can feel it in my hand. Rough and dangerous edges.
Impending destruction...and death.

                                JOHN
Of course.

                                DAVE
And you? You try, John.

                                JOHN
(flips coin) Smooth, Dave. Safe. Polished. Shining and golden.

                                DAVE
Incredible, John.

                                JOHN
Perspective, Dave.

                                DAVE
OK. Let me do this one.

(DAVE grabs the cardboard French fry tray)

This thing is rectangular—like a prison cell. And it's smashed in, dented on one side—which is
like injury, like being crushed—

                                JOHN
--Dave, what are you doing?

                                DAVE
Well, the last French fry is me in a prison cell...and—

                                JOHN
Dave, that's just a piece of cardboard. It's nothing. It's garbage.

                                DAVE
But I thought—

                                JOHN
Really, Dave. You'd better settle down. I mean, get a hold of yourself. Take a breath.

                                DAVE
You're right, John. What's wrong with me? I'm teetering. I'm on the edge.

                                JOHN
You're on the threshold, Dave. There's a new world out there for you, Dave. You're Magellan
navigating the world. You're Columbus discovering America. You're Jeff Bezos discovering the
Amazon. Explore, Dave. Sail away. Picture yourself at sea, Dave. Feel the swell of the ocean.
Hear the billowing sails. Listen, Dave. Do you hear?

                                DAVE
I hear nothing, John. I feel nothing. I mean, what's happened to me, John? Explain it to me.

JOHN

Look, Dave. We'll try a different approach. You're all tense. You've got to learn to relax with this whole thing.

DAVE

What do you mean—relax?

JOHN

Sure. Relax. Now close your eyes—

DAVE

John—

JOHN

I want you to close your eyes—and concentrate only on the sound of my voice. (pause) That's it. Now I want you to relate to me in detail the last dream you had—

DAVE

--Really, John—

JOHN

--Just do as I say. Tell me all about it. Remember: keep your eyes closed.

> (At this point, JOHN carefully stands and moves upstage, away from the table. He takes out his cell phone, calls someone, and carries on a phone conversation, completely ignoring DAVE as he narrates his dream.)

DAVE
> (DAVE, with eyes closed, recounts his dream.)

Well, John, now that you bring it up, I did have this strange dream the other night. I was sitting in some theater—like in the audience. So, we're all watching what looks to be…a magic act. There's a magician, all dressed in black. The big hat. The cape. Everything. And he had this assistant. A beautiful blond woman. And there was this box. You know. The box they use to cut a lady in half. That sort of thing. But then this strange thing happened.

> (Sometime, in the middle of DAVE's account. JOHN, still on the phone, appears to look for something, and then moves offstage. He returns a minute later chewing on a hotdog, still on the phone, still not listening to his friend.)

How can I describe it? The woman. She climbs into the box, all right, but before she does, she takes off her clothes. I mean, all of them. And the magician does the same thing. He climbs into the box with the woman. I mean, right there on stage. Meanwhile, we in the audience are hushed. We can only wait and stare at the whole thing. And we wait. And we wait for what seems like hours, days, weeks. Well, it turns out it must have been a lot longer than that— because out of the box comes this sound. It's the whimpering sound of a new-born baby—and these arms emerge from the box. The arms are holding the baby up for the audience to see. Then the smiling woman sits up with her baby. The magician—he hops out of the box and takes this giant bow. The audience by now is going wild—cheering, clapping. And me. I'm cheering and clapping along with everybody else. (Pause) We give them a standing ovation.

> (JOHN returns quietly to his seat, having missed DAVE's entire account. DAVE opens his eyes.)

DAVE, Cont.
Wasn't that something, John? What do you think?

JOHN
What do <u>you</u> think, Dave? That's the important thing.

DAVE
Well, I'm not sure how to think about the magic, but maybe, in a way, I'm like a baby—a new-born baby.

JOHN
--There you go. Happy Birthday, Dave.

DAVE
John, you know something? I feel better. I feel good. I kind of feel—like what you said—I feel like I'm on the threshold...the threshold of possibilities.

JOHN
Absolutely, Dave. And now is the time and the moment is pregnant with possibilities.

DAVE
Oh yes. I can feel it. And you're right, John. The moment <u>is</u> pregnant. How can I thank you, John?

JOHN
Don't thank <u>me</u>, Dave. You got the moment pregnant. I just watched.

DAVE
I really can't thank you enough, John. You know, it's so refreshing that in this day and age two grown men can get together and communicate on this level—

JOHN
(JOHN has been checking the time, distracted)

What? What did you say, Dave?

DAVE
I said it's refreshing that two men can communicate on a level of deep friendship—

JOHN
--Dave, you're going to have to excuse me. You have another beer or something. I have to run. My wife and I are having dinner guests tonight.

DAVE
Oh, I'm sorry I kept you, John. Hope you're not too late.

JOHN
No. It's all right. It's just Frank and Carol. Anyway, gotta run, buddy. Take care.

(JOHN exits.)
DAVE
Right, John. And you take care, too, my friend. (a pause to consider) Frank?...Frank Hennesy?

end

Superpeople

David Capps

New Haven, CT

Ah superpeople, superpeople! Not only Yalies
looking down at their cellphones as they walk,
with their amazing core-strength, capable of
bouncing back any slight with the extreme
repel of an industrial hydraulic press chipping
the centers of alloys till they burst and bleed.
No, not only Yalies, but the management, so
articulate, not texting, but talking as they walk,
at the one end of a business deal you never
know, who could be the next Big Deal, and if
anything seems amiss, out of place, less than
clear, not quite well articulated, impractical,
puzzling, mysterious, questionable, down-right
wrong, savage, glaring, inopportune, transient,
uneducated, unworthy, sentimental, opposed,
too unopposed, melancholic, ill-suited to being
in their way. Well, they won't let you know
the love they know from fables of their lives.

Zelda, Before Daisy

Andrew Graber

Bedtime Story

Daniel P. Stokes

You washed. I waited reading.
You emerged. "You'll turn the lamp off,
won't you, very soon?" I grunted,
constrained again to follow my intent.
Kissed fingers touched my forehead.
Heard a slipper, then the other, shed.
But second leg *en route* towards the sheets
you stopped a-straddle, perched,
mouth pursed in concentration, buttocks clenched.
To no avail.
Out sparked a ping,
A single syllabyled contracted fart.
Your eyes above your hand dilated
and you gasped, "Oh!"
The stench was noxious, sour,
pervasive; I shook the sheet
to waft it elsewhere, and you,
you skipped – a schoolgirl giggling –
to the toilet. That's it,
I told myself, that's it.
The honeymoon is over.

Conflagration

One-Act Play
Richard Lehan

SETTING

    The Parting Glass, Beacon Street, Boston. Early evening.

    Two men are sitting side-by-side at the bar looking out at the audience throughout the play. An overhead light makes them the focal point on the stage, although a BARTENDER will move in and out.

    Seated on the left is MARTIN CURRAN, a 61-year-old partner at a law firm located across the street from the pub. In the stool next to him is KYLE BETTENCOURT, a 32-year-old associate at the same firm who has worked with Martin on several matters. Both men are wearing dark suits. Martin has loosened the tie around his neck, while KYLE carefully folded and placed his tie in the briefcase at his feet before the action of the play begins. The pint glass on the bar in front of Martin is empty except for the foam that unevenly coats the inside of the glass. KYLE's pint glass is about a quarter full.

MARTIN
(emphatically)

Boylan's a fucking nitwit, Kyle. I learned that early on.

KYLE
(exasperated)

I get that he's the partner but it's going to end up biting the two of us in the ass with the client.

MARTIN

Well, yeah. I know from experience. Early in my career, this client calls me all wound up after reviewing my billable hours: "Counsel! If I ask you to dig a grave, you only need to dig six feet down!"

KYLE
(erupts in laughter, then looks at Martin out of the corner of his eye.)

By the way, Peter thinks you're a prick.

MARTIN

That's old news, Kyle. Boylan and I started as associates at the same time and we've been butting heads ever since.

                              KYLE
        (resigned)

I just know he'd throw me under the bus in a heartbeat.

                              MARTIN
Guaranteed. Never let your guard down around that asshole.

        (Martin surveys the empty pint glasses in front of them.)

Time for another round? The next train for me...

        (He pulls back his sleeve to look at his watch.)

...isn't for another hour plus.

                              KYLE
        (In contrast, KYLE checks the time by tapping his phone in front of him on the bar.)

Sure, why not. I can hop on the Red Line at any time.

        (He drains the rest of his glass.)

                              MARTIN
Good. I got this.

        (He catches the attention of the unseen bartender by pointing two fingers at the empty
        pint glasses.)

                              KYLE
Again?

                              MARTIN
Please, I'm delaying the start of your weekend.

                              KYLE
No, you're kicking it off!

        (The BARTENDER enters from stage left with two new pints and exits in the same
        direction with the empty glasses.)

                              MARTIN
        (raising his glass slightly)

Slainte!

                              KYLE
        (raises his glass, too)

Cheers to closing out another week in the books.

MARTIN
(after taking a drink from his pint)

I've got a shitload more books behind me than you do, Kyle.

KYLE
(smirking)

Yeah, and it shows.

MARTIN
(ruefully)

And I've got the shrapnel to prove it.

(KYLE chuckles. Satisfied, MARTIN takes a sip from his pint.)

Did you know that I've been commuting into Boston by train for over thirty years? One hour each way.

KYLE
My God, what's that been like?

MARTIN
(thoughtfully)

Honestly? Most of the time, it's like being trapped in a reoccurring dream. You wouldn't know one year from the next but for the change in seasons.

KYLE
Yeah, the subway's starting to feel that way for me, too.

MARTIN
In fairness, I always get a seat on the morning train into town. That gives me a head start on my emails and time to peruse the newspaper.

(Something in KYLE's expression prompts MARTIN to respond with mock defensiveness.)

I'm a dinosaur, Kyle! I refuse to read the *Globe* on my phone.

KYLE
(affectionately)

To each his own, boss.

MARTIN
My point is that driving into Boston is not a viable option.

KYLE

No question about that.

> (He takes a drink from his pint before continuing.)

The subway is nothing to crow about either. The Green Line's on life support; I end up standing the whole way down to Park Street every morning. The only advantage is that I'm not tied to a train schedule like you. That would suck even more.

MARTIN

It's not an issue for me during the workweek but take tonight as an example. The next train's not until 8:37, which means I won't be home before 10:15 tonight.

KYLE

At least it's Friday.

MARTIN

> (He carefully clinks his mostly full pint glass against KYLE's stationary glass.)

TGIF.

> (There is a lull in their conversation as they both stare straight ahead. After a pause of about five seconds, MARTIN takes a sip from his pint. KYLE does the same.)

MARTIN

Yup, there's a sameness to commuting by train; one ride blurs into another.

> (The expression on his face undergoes a subtle change.)

But...then comes the rare occasion when the unexpected happens and it turns into a story.

KYLE

> (glances over at MARTIN)

Okay.

MARTIN

> (nodding as he speaks)

And I got a train story for you, brother.

> (He takes a long pull from his pint glass.)

You up for it?

KYLE

Proceed, counsel.

MARTIN

> (deferentially)

Thank you, your honor.

> (clears throat)

MARTIN, Cont.
So. This happened to me at the close of summer two years ago.

(He pauses to retrieve the specific day from his memory.)

The Thursday before the Labor Day weekend. You remember how hot that summer was, right? There was no relief from the scorching temperatures for, like, three weeks.

KYLE
(thinking for a moment)

Ok, not this past summer, but the one before that…yeah, I was staying on the Vineyard that week with my then girlfriend…sure, I recall it being quite warm, even on the island.

MARTIN
Well, it was horrendous here in town. You could wring the moisture out of the air.

(takes a sip from his pint)

I was in Back Bay for a morning meeting with the Authority at their attorneys' firm in the Prudential Center. This was in my role as bond counsel for the Commonwealth. We were putting together another revenue bond offering to finance the Authority's sewer infrastructure work.

KYLE
(sees an opening)

Hey Marty, I'd like to work with you on one of those deals sometime…

MARTIN
That can be arranged; they'll be a few more before I retire.

(MARTIN takes another sip from his pint before continuing with his story.)

Anyways, it ended up being a productive meeting—with lunch provided as the standard perk.

(As an aside)

Give me a tuna club, bag of chips, and a big chocolate chip cookie and I'm good.

Afterwards, I decided to walk to Bay Bay Station and catch an early train home. To avoid the heat, I traversed that glassed-in connector bridge to the adjoining Copley Square mall. Exit from there and you're a stone's throw from the station.

KYLE
Sure, I've done that…in the dead of winter, too.

MARTIN
Right, right. Me, too. When I got to the station there was a smattering of people waiting on the underground platform for the Providence Local to arrive from South Station. Talk about hot: I remember the sweat sealing my shirt against my back.

KYLE
You weren't wearing a suit, were you?

MARTIN

No! I wore a tie to the meeting, but the minute it broke up, the tie ended up in the bottom of my briefcase. Wouldn't you know that my guy, the Undersecretary for Administration and Finance, came dressed to the meeting in his favorite pinstripe suit. Thinks he's David Niven.

> (KYLE doesn't get MARTIN's reference to an actor from an older generation; after a beat, Martin takes another sip from his pint.)

There I am stuck on this oven-like platform, waiting and waiting, until—finally—a double-decker train rumbles to a stop in front of me. My first thought was: God, I hope the air conditioner's working. Because that's a crap shoot, too. But once I entered the bottom-level car, I was hit with a gush of the cool air...

> (MARTIN exhales a deep breath.)

KYLE

Halleluiah.

MARTIN

Felt like I hit the lottery...for once. It being an early afternoon train, I had my choice of empty two-seaters and decided on a window seat—one of the ones that face backwards from the train engine.

KYLE

That doesn't bother you?

MARTIN

Nah, never has.

KYLE

Ok, sorry to interrupt.

MARTIN

That's fine. Yeah, so after the train departed Back Bay, I took out my phone and began going through emails. The next stop was Ruggles where only a handful of people got on. Once we were underway, the conductor comes through the car checking tickets. "Got ya," he says when I held up my train pass to him. All the way to the end of the car, he drones: "Got ya...got ya...got ya..."

KYLE

Like a broken record...

MARTIN

Exactly.

> (He takes one sip from his pint and continues.)

As the train headed toward the Route 128 station, I opened up a redline version of the R.O. bond offering produced by the Authority's counsel. He had walked us through his draft at the meeting, but now I wanted to flyspeck the actual language. I had to turn the phone sideways like this to get a wider view...

> (MARTIN illustrates for KYLE by using the index finger and thumb on both hands to frame an imaginary phone.)

MARTIN (Cont.)
Then I used my finger to slowly swipe through the pages.

(His left index finger swipes at the air front of KYLE.)

KYLE
(Bemused)

You figured that out all by yourself, Curran?

MARTIN
Wiseass. So, I'm scrolling through one marked-up page to the next when I start to hear the faint sound of a helicopter. It barely registered at first, but then the whirling blades kept getting louder and closer and louder...

KYLE
(takes a sip from his pint as a smile creases his face)

Hey, remember the Huey crisscrossing the screen at the beginning of Apocalypse Now? Thunka-Thunka-Thunka. I watched it again on Netflix the other night.

MARTIN
Huh?

(It takes a beat for MARTIN to orient himself.)

Ok, yeah. Great film. I saw Apocalypse Now on the big screen when it first came out in 1979. Like three times. Did you know that Coppola originally wanted Steve McQueen to play the role of Willard?

KYLE
No kidding.

MARTIN
Yeah. I mean Martin Sheen was very good, but McQueen...with Brando? That would have been something, huh?

KYLE
Epic.

MARTIN
But we digress.

(He glances over at his pint but holds off taking a drink.)

So, without taking my eyes off the phone, I thought: hmmm, there's a helicopter hovering over us - that's... unusual.

KYLE
Could you see it from the window?

MARTIN

(shakes his head)

My eyes were still glued to the phone. Next, I heard two guys talking down at the other end of the car but couldn't make out what they were saying. At that point, I had only a couple of more pages of redlines to review. All of a sudden, one of them yells: "Whoa!" and my head instinctively swiveled from the phone to the window.

(He twists his head over his left shoulder.)

And what I saw - ok? – what my eyes beheld - was a massive fire up ahead.

(KYLE's eyes widen.)

MARTIN, Cont.

You heard me.

KYLE

How big?

MARTIN

A conflagration - that's how big.

(He takes a gulp from his pint.)

KYLE

Jesus. But explain to me -

MARTIN

(cuts KYLE off)

Picture this: In normal weather, the track runs alongside a field of wetlands that stretch as far back as the eye can see. But the heat wave had turned the wetlands into acres of prime kindling—now all ablaze in a fiery spiral.

(As he speaks, MARTIN's hand lifts from the bar in a spiral.*)*

From what I could tell, there was no more than, say, fifteen yards separating the track from the flames.

KYLE

(drinks from his pint)

Shit. That's crazy.

MARTIN

Not only that, but the train...slowed down.

KYLE

(begins slowly shaking his head)

MARTIN

Wait for it. And then—then, like thirty seconds later, the train jerked to a full stop right alongside this curtain of fire. If the AC had shut down at that moment, the car would have turned into a giant Hot Pocket inside of ten minutes.

KYLE
(laughs, and then imitates Jim Gaffigan in a sing-song voice)

Hot Poc-kets!

(KYLE takes another drink from his pint.)

Where was the conductor?

MARTIN

Made himself scarce, of course. By then, the chopper had retreated. The other passengers were jabbering and pointing their phones at the windows. All of us were waiting for some kind of explanation. Meanwhile, the fire running the length of the windows in the car looked like a mammoth, badass screen-saver. It was probably a good thirty seconds before the conductor's voice wafted from the intercom.

(MARTIN speaks with an exaggerated Boston accent.)

May I have your attention please. There is a problem with the signal coming into the Route 128 station. The train engineer is awaiting clearance to move forward. We expect to be underway momentarily.

KYLE
(incredulous)

Just a signal problem, folks. Ha!

MARTIN

I kid you not. Nice touch, Mr. Conductor, foregoing any mention of the inferno threatening to incinerate our train. And I knew from experience that the conductor's promise that we would be underway...

(MARTIN makes air quotes with his fingers)

"momentarily" was code for "settle in for a wait, passengers."

(He pauses to take another drink from his pint.)

I'm thinking: is this really how my summer's going to end? The summer where I took, like, two vacation days. All at once I felt utterly spent, like the last residue of energy escaped from my body and dissolved into thin air.

I knew I was too on edge to fall asleep...

KYLE
(interjects)

Ya think?!

MARTIN

(chuckles)

...but closed my eyes anyways and leaned back in the seat, the phone still in my hand. From there, my mind powered down to a fuzzy-black screen for maybe another minute or so...

(MARTIN pauses before continuing with a hint of hesitation.)

then, ah - without any forethought on my part—a vivid memory of my dad materialized before me.

KYLE

(with a look of mild surprise)

Huh.

MARTIN

I know—like where did that come from? Now, my dad had died eight months earlier, but...

KYLE

(Interrupts)

I never heard about that, Marty.

MARTIN

No? That's ok. It wasn't sudden, Kyle. My father had pancreatic cancer. He was receiving palliative care within five months of his diagnosis.

KYLE

Hospice?

MARTIN

Yeah, at home...a nurse would come by a few times a week and administer morphine for the pain.

KYLE

Damn. How old was your dad when he died, Marty?

MARTIN

(calculates in his head)

Let's see... 83...yeah, he would have turned 84 that March.

KYLE

What was his name?

MARTIN

Timothy...Tim.

KYLE

You know, in thinking about the timing, I had probably just started at the firm. In any event, the word never filtered down to me...my very belated condolences, Marty.

MARTIN

No worries, Kyle. I was back at work the day after his funeral.

(He takes a sip from his pint.)

Okay, so I'm sitting on the train: exhausted—resting my eyes—waiting for us to move out of danger—and a memory of what turned out to be my last visit with the old man popped into my head out of the blue. It was like I pressed "play" on a video running behind my eyelids.

KYLE

Weird...well, not weird but unexpected; I mean given the circumstances.

MARTIN

No, you're right, Kyle; it was weird. Now, the visit with my dad occurred over the Martin Luther King holiday weekend, the Saturday. That's partly why I can put a date to it.

KYLE

Sure.

MARTIN

I had planned to stop in over the long weekend, but I hadn't decided which day. After breakfast, I worked straight through the morning...playing catch-up, as usual.

KYLE

Tell me about it.

MARTIN

I told Maureen after lunch: You know what? I'm going to get a coffee and swing by the folks' house.

KYLE

Same house you grew up in?

MARTIN

Yeah, in Canton.

KYLE

Believe it or not, my parents have already downsized to a condo in Providence.

MARTIN

Good for them.

KYLE

It's strange, though. I have no childhood home to go back to.

MARTIN

Trust me, Kyle, you'll thank them for their foresight.

Anyways, that Saturday was shit-cold. The wind chill dropped the temperature into the single digits. When I got to the house, a gust buffeted me against the side door as I fumbled with the key to gain entry into the kitchen. Inside, it was as warm as toast. My mother kept the heat up to like 75 degrees all the time.

KYLE

Oh man, that's way too warm for me.

Me, too, but it felt wonderful coming in from outside. The first thing I did was grab a bottle of vanilla Ensure from the refrigerator for my dad. He needed a straw to get it down and I found one in the overhead cabinet. Coming out of the kitchen, I could see him lying on his side in the hospital bed that been moved into the front room. He appeared to be sleeping, so I headed upstairs to look for my mom. I found her in their bedroom lying on top of the made bed with her arms folded across her chest. If rosary beads had been entwined in her hands, you would have thought she was in her casket.

(MARTIN, noticing the expression on KYLE's face, responds.)

Yeah, it was morbid thought on my part, but there it was.

(He drinks from his pint; KYLE takes a sip from his.)

MARTIN

Dad was sitting up on the side of the bed when I came downstairs, and he greeted me with a weak salute.

(MARTIN half salutes KYLE.)

Slouched over like a puppet, weighing no more than 120 pounds by then.

KYLE

That's tough to see.

MARTIN

You get used to it. I sat next to him on the bed, practically shoulder to shoulder.

I spoke first:

Mom's still napping upstairs so I let her be.

Good, he rasped, good; she needs a respite. I'm running her ragged.

Mom's happy to do it, Dad.

She didn't sign up for this.

Your bride would tell you: I damn well did.

I tapped him on the knee. Now I want to hear how you're doing.

Very worn out, Martin, he says, shaking his head.

What have you eaten today?

Your mother boiled me an egg for breakfast. I spent ten minutes chipping the shell off before handing it back to her as bald as me.

(MARTIN chuckles at the memory of his dad's remark.)

I handed the Ensure with the straw in it to him and said: Alright, Dad, try to drink as much of this as you can.

He cradled the bottle in his hands, both of which were tattooed with blood-bruises, while one hand of mine supported his back. I could feel his knobby spine protruding under my palm.

Dad tugged dutifully on the straw a few times before shaking his head - meaning "enough." As I took the bottle back, he turned to face me.

(MARTIN takes a sip from his pint.)

MARTIN

Do you know what I saw, Kyle?

KYLE

What?

MARTIN

(quietly)

A look of bare acceptance.

KYLE

(beginning to feel awkward)

That, ah--

MARTIN

(eyes fixed ahead)

Then my dad cleared his throat and said:

Thank you, son, for keeping me company.

Of course, Dad, of course.

You're still my best boyo, you know.

Never doubted it, Dad, I answered back.

(MARTIN glances down to find both hands gripping his pint glass before continuing.)

And here's the thing: I knew in that moment that our exchange was his reticent way of saying goodbye to me... but I didn't have the poise or words to acknowledge it as such.

KYLE

Don't be too hard on yourself, buddy.

MARTIN
(taking another sip from his pint)

I'm not; it's the truth—I couldn't reciprocate…and, let's see, the following Wednesday morning—very early because Maureen and I were still in bed—my mom's number came up on my phone and I knew he was gone.

MARTIN
(He pauses before finishing off the rest of his pint.)

So, after barely thinking about my father since his death, he paid me a visit right there on the train.

(With effort, MARTIN makes eye contact with KYLE.)

It overwhelmed me, Kyle…and I…well, I broke down.

KYLE
(uncertain on how to respond)

Ok…that happens, Marty, emotions can sneak up on you…

MARTIN
And bowl you over, Kyle. I heard myself start to sob. One hand clenched my phone; the other was balled into a fist.

(He illustrates with both hands; his eyes glisten recalling the image.)

KYLE
(after pausing to collect his thoughts)

Now, I can't speak from personal experience about a death of a parent because mine are in good health—knock on wood.

MARTIN
(recovers by responding sarcastically)

Kyle, they're probably younger than I am.

KYLE
Might be. But to finish my thought—I think back to what happened to my mom and me when I was—what?—eight years old at the time. Even though it's probably not analogous to your experience, but still…

MARTIN
That's alright.

KYLE
Anyways, the first thing you have to understand about my mom is that she's very strong, stoic even. She was the disciplinarian in the family. Her and my older sister, Carla, fought all the time. My dad was more easygoing, but in fairness to my mom she was at home with us all day.

MARTIN
So, her full-time job was putting up with you—that's cruel and unusual punishment.

KYLE

(chuckles)

I was an angel compared to my sister. Actually, my mom's a CPA but only worked part-time while I was in elementary school.

MARTIN

Ok. My mom didn't return to work as a telephone operator until I was in middle school. I get what you're saying.

KYLE

Right. So, this was the summer before I started third grade. I was coming back from my best friend's house after playing outside all afternoon, but now it was time for supper, you know? As I crossed the street in front of our home, I spotted my mom standing alone on the side lawn with her back to me. And on a whim, really, I decided to sneak up on her from behind...I literally moved toward her on tiptoes, and she didn't hear me coming. When I got close enough, I reached out and tagged her—lightly—on the back.

(KYLE's index finger dabs at the air in front of him.)

...and, I mean, she jumped!

MARTIN

Was she on the phone or something? Wait, were cordless phones even around then?

KYLE

No, no.

(He clears his throat.)

I really startled her...and when she swung around, her face was streaked with tears. Now, I had never seen my mother cry. I couldn't even imagine such a thing. It shocked me, and I blurted out—it was almost like a plea: 'what's wrong, Ma?!' She just shook her head at me and couldn't speak.

MARTIN

That must have been disconcerting.

KYLE

I ran into the house without another word. I found Carla watching TV in the rec room where she informed me in a solemn, big sister voice that our nana from the Azores had passed away. 'How?' I asked. Carla didn't sugarcoat it: 'she dropped dead from a heart attack that morning while fixing breakfast for papa.' I didn't know how to react; it was my first experience with a death in the family. The truth is neither my sister nor I knew our Azores grandparents very well; we didn't see them enough. But the shock it gave my mom discombobulated me. I retreated to my bedroom and shut the door. Sprawled on the bed staring up at the ceiling, I pictured my mom's contorted face again and started bawling my eyes out.

(KYLE looks MARTIN square in the face and exclaims)

Jesus, Curran! What kind of mojo are you conjuring up here tonight?

MARTIN

(chuckles)

Courtesy of our bartender...for medicinal purposes only. Seriously, though, your mom was reacting in real time to her mother's sudden death, and you were a kid trying to process it all.

(sheepishly)

But I was, like, 58 or 59 at the time, months removed from my father's expected death from cancer.

KYLE

You still have nothing to be embarrassed about, Marty.

(He pauses to take a drink from his pint.)

Everyone grieves on their own timeline.

(It hits KYLE how cliched that sounds, and he adds)

Not to oversimplify it...

MARTIN

(smiles indulgently)

I'll go with that, Kyle.

Meanwhile, embarrassed as I was, I couldn't stop crying. The other passengers probably thought I was having a panic attack because of the fire.

KYLE

Fuck'em.

MARTIN

There you go. I was half-expecting the conductor to show up at any moment demanding an explanation for my disruptive conduct.

(MARTIN laughs softly; KYLE joins in.)

But he never did. I was drying my eyes with the tie I retrieved from my briefcase when the Amtrak train from DC roared past us on the outside track into Boston. Right on cue, our train hitched forward as the conductor got back on the intercom.

(MARTIN speaks in his conductor-voice again)

Next stop, Route 128 station. Please exit the train only where you see a conductor. We apologize for any inconvenience.

KYLE

Nothing out of the ordinary here, people...

MARTIN

This is it.

KYLE

How long were you stuck there?

MARTIN

I don't know, probably less than fifteen minutes. I watched the fire recede from my vision as the train pulled into the Route 128 station. From there, we proceeded without a hitch to my stop in Mansfield.

(MARTIN watches KYLE take a drink from his pint.)

Remember the helicopter hovering overhead? That night, Channel 5 showed aerial footage of my train acting as an impromptu firewall. Surreal.

KYLE

(glances at his phone to check the time)

You had yourself quite an adventure, Mr. Curran.

MARTIN

(taps his finger on the bar)

To complete the story, I took next day off and the first thing I did was visit my dad's grave. There's a plaque honoring his service in the Navy during World War II, but it had sunk unevenly in the ground, and the overgrown grass had obscured some of the lettering. I spent the next ten minutes pulling up the wet grass with my bare hands to make it look respectable.

KYLE

See, you are a good son.

(KYLE glances at his pint glass, which is still almost half full, and decides to leave it.)

MARTIN

(with a clouded look on his face)

Do you know what else I regret, Kyle?

KYLE

I don't...

MARTIN

I never told that story to my mom. It's too late now. After my dad died, she declined so quickly—physically and memory-wise—that I had to put her in a nursing home. For her own safety really...

Whenever I visit her these days, one of the aides—usually Jody—escorts me down to her room. And every time my mom sees us come through the door, her eyes shine—but at Jody, not me.

KYLE

(He stands up with his brief case in one hand and addresses MARTIN before extending his hand.)

Man, you got all kinds of shrapnel.

MARTIN
(shakes KYLE's hand while remaining seated)

Hey, I'm willing to have a sidebar with Boylan, if you think it would help...one partner to another...

KYLE
(certain that would be counterproductive)

I appreciate the offer, Marty, but I'm good. Have a good weekend.

MARTIN
Okay, you too...we're back at it on Monday, brother.

(KYLE exits stage right. After a beat of silence, MARTIN checks his watch, then takes out a credit card from his wallet to catch the eye of the unseen bartender with it.)

(Blackout)

Lonely School

Duane L Herrmann

Of hewn stone,
rock solid,
with good roof,
essential
for preservation
of any building,
yet, not enough
when culture changes
and people move
far enough away
to not return;
now sitting alone
no trees or playground,
surrounded, close,
by inches,
to acres of wheat,
abandoned,
no further use.

Awakening

Karen Colstrom

Language's Fecundity

Loralee Clark

She extends her limbs by pumping her heart
(ancient trick of patience)
as she prepares her web,
extruding the liquid silk from spinnerets.
This hardens in the air as she begins to weave
a sturdy trap to carry for casting out
and reeling in, inconspicuous as breath.

In grocery stores *cucumber* and *guacamole* are expected
but sometimes she comes away with prizes like
excruciating sympathies.

Wednesdays are for economic classes:
sectors, recidivism, paradigm or a phrase
artificially produced scarcity.

She skulks through late hours for *loneliness,
supersede,* and *paraplegic.*

Once she has the words safe in her web
she draws them into her chelicerae, past the pedipalps
to digest and taste energy in *liverwort, monocot, lichens, symbiotic;*
smoke and earthiness of *Uruk* or *delicate alders,*
sharp bitterness of *archaea* and *cyanobacteria.*

She wonders if we could plait webs would we snatch
useless items in a market stall, money at a bank,
or would we parachute away from ourselves and circumstance;
we walk through life not realizing language's sustenance:
just this week she has partaken of earth apples
and the plague of fellow-feelings,
sections of a circle and habits of relapsing,
the condition of being solitary as well as postponement.

One word is a pomegranate: full of enough seeds
to sow an entire orchard.

Choice

One-Act Play
Allison Whittenberg

CHARACTERS
      WANDA 30ish Black woman, humbly dressed
      HELEN Wanda's sister, flashily dressed
      SOCIAL WORKER (heard only by phone)
      ASHLEY and BRITTNEY (two girls always off stage)

SETTING
      Kitchen of an apartment. Present day.

(WANDA drinks coffee and reads the morning newspaper. The phone rings.)

SOCIAL WORKER (off stage)

Hello, Miss Phillips; how are Brittany and Alicia?

WANDA

Ashley's fine too.

SOCIAL WORKER (off stage)

Oh, I'm sorry; I meant that. How are you?

WANDA

I'm fine. How are you?

SOCIAL WORKER(off stage)

I'm fine.

WANDA

Good.

SOCIAL WORKER(off stage)

Good.

(WANDA sips her coffee and glances at the end of section B, the obituary page.)

SOCIAL WORKER (off stage)

Their mother had another, Miss Phillips. Another girl. It was born two days ago. It has all ten fingers and all ten toes.

WANDA

How did she get pregnant again? I thought she was in jail.

SOCIAL WORKER (off stage)

She is.

WANDA

She's in jail and pregnant?

SOCIAL WORKER (off stage)

She gave birth. I really hate calling you. I hate telling you this.

WANDA

How could you let that happen?

SOCIAL WORKER (off stage)

I'm really the middle man.

WANDA

I can't take on another child.

SOCIAL WORKER (off stage)

You don't have to decide this minute. Why don't I call you in a few days?

WANDA

Where is she now?

SOCIAL WORKER (off stage)

In jail.

WANDA

No, the baby.

SOCIAL WORKER (off stage)

The facility has temporary housing for –

WANDA

That's a sin. The baby is in custody?

SOCIAL WORKER (off stage)

Miss Phillips, this is the way things work.

WANDA

How could you let this happen?

SOCIAL WORKER (off stage)

Please, I almost didn't call, but I thought you should know. Miss Phillips, I'm giving you too much at once. I'll call you back in a few days.

SCENE 2

WANDA (to the audience)

I work in a gray building filing papers. There, when phones ring, I answer them.

We look alike, my adopted children and me. The rich mocha and cocoa hues of my skin matched theirs. They look like childhood pictures of me and my sister with our wide brimmed noses, rust colored plaits, and genetic trademarks.

Four could live as cheaply as three, right? Right? What's another pair of school shoes, more money for milk, another college fund? I should take in that child. I have to. I kept my hair short, but I straightened it. I wear slacks most days, not skirts because I don't have the time to fuss with leg shaving and panty hose.

I haven't had a date in two years, but it's not my kids' fault. I never dated much before them.

Brittany came addicted: underweight, about as heavy as a shadow, shaking, ashy complexioned. I sat up with her many a night trying to undo what had been done to her while she lived in someone else's womb. I didn't choose to have Ashley one year later. If it was up to me, I would have spaced them in a three years span. I got Ashley at two weeks and even then, she looked stunted and underdeveloped.

So, now six years later, there's an addition. Ashley has trouble sleeping. What would it be like with a crying baby in the house?

Babies are so easy to love. They are so small and helpless looking and have limited emotional range: they laugh and cry easily and are entertained with animal quilts and balloons and monotonous music.

(HELEN enters the room.)

HELEN

Her tubes should be cut, and they should be fried.

WANDA

The child is already here.

HELEN

Then let Steven Spielberg adopt it. He likes our people. He's a millionaire. You're a secretary, barely making 43 a year. He has an estate. You have a lousy apartment.

> (HELEN sits as WANDA unpacks the groceries and sits as WANDA puts away the groceries and sits as WANDA begins making supper.)

HELEN

Stop trying to save the whole goddamn world.

WANDA

Do you have to put it like that, Helen?

HELEN

What, you want to be like everyone else? So PC that I'm not saying anything. Look, I voted in the last election. I serve on juries. I pay taxes on time. I've even given the Red Cross a whole freaking, fracking pint of my blood. I'm a good person.

WANDA

They aren't the kind of girls where a lot of strangers would coo over. I don't think Steven Spielberg is the answer.

HELEN

Why didn't this woman have an abortion? At least with an abortion, you know it's over. Shit, doesn't it bother her not knowing what happened to this little girl?

HELEN

I can't leave her there.

WANDA

Why not? She's not yours. You keep messing around and you're going to be like those people on <u>20/20</u>, They got a kid from each country. Shit. It's not your problem. Have them call up one of those Scientologists. Are you crying?

HELEN

No, I'm just slicing onions.

> (HELEN gets up and takes the knife from WANDA's hands. She begins chopping, without tears or remorse.)

HELEN

Do you want to hear a joke?

WANDA

Right now?

HELEN

Yep.

WANDA

No, I'm not really in the mood to laugh.

HELEN

You'll like this one because it has a moral.

WANDA

Shoot.

HELEN

Jesus is sitting around the table with the apostles, and he asks Paul, 'Paul, what do you bring?' Paul says, 'Sorry, Jesus, I forgot.' Then Jesus turns to John and asks, 'John, What did you bring?' And John says, 'I'm sorry, I didn't bring anything.' So Jesus says, 'Okay, apostles, you have done this to me time and time again: This is your last supper.'...You see, even Jesus had His limits.

(The phone rings. WANDA goes to pick it up.)

SOCIAL WORKER (off stage)

Miss Philips?

WANDA

You said you would give me a few days.

BRITTANY (off stage)

Mommy, who is it?

HELEN

Is it --

SOCIAL WORKER (off stage)

Miss Phillips, I know, but I really want to move on this. We can arrange to have you take the child –

WANDA

I'm not going to do it. Find another home for her.

BRITTANY (Off Stage)

W-w-who's h-her, Mommy?

HELEN

Brittany, be quiet.

SOCIAL WORKER (off stage)

Are you sure you don't need more time to think about it?

ASHLEY (off stage)

Who's Mommy talking to?

WANDA

I can't. I can't. I can not do this. Again. (to HELEN) Helen, could you keep the girls in the other room?

HELEN

(leaving the room)
You're doing the right thing.

SOCIAL WORKER (off stage)

I really shouldn't be saying this, but there is no other place for her. I've tried. No other place...

You can name this one. Miss Phillips --

(WANDA hangs up the phone. BLACKOUT.)

Love Is a Little Demon

Natalie Castagnola

Love is a little demon
that sits inside me, at the pit of my stomach.
Glutinous and ravenous.
It feasts on the drippings of the fatty tallow of my desperation.

My little demon cannot survive on fat alone.
It doesn't desire to feel merely satiated,
it craves protein.
It wants to grow.
To take.
Red meat.

My little demon gnaws and scratches at my insides.
Furious by what I seem to be denying it.
Pounding its angry fists against my lower belly,
rebelling against my own body for not giving it what it wants.
My little demon works much like a uterus in that way.

"More! More! You alone are not enough!" it wails from the depths of my bowels.
It has been too hungry for too long.
It needs others.

This is what I mean when I say I have so much love to give.

Dreams of Home

Karen Colstrom

If I Had Been With You Then

Diane Zoeller

If I had been with you then
I would have felt the ceaseless ocean swells
that marked your passage
in the dark bowels of the ship
that brought you here

You, at six years old, were given milk
that soured with each sip
a taste that stayed with you into old age

If I had been with you then
I would have shared your wonder
as you entered New York harbor
I would have sat on the bench with you at Ellis Island
You, in your threadbare clothing
shivering in the winter cold

If I had known you then
I would have laughed when
you listened intently to the Yiddish spoken
in your neighborhood, thinking you were learning
your first English words

I would have seen your mother
caring for seven children
scrubbing the steps of the apartment building in Brooklyn
which by miracle she came to own
She, fending off the Black Hand when they threatened
And hiding you from their grasp

I would have known you
when you went to work at the garment factory
toiling at your sewing machine
Then raising a son by yourself
in an age that held room for no such thing

I knew you when you were already old
after losing three husbands
to infidelity, death, abandonment

Yet still, you had looked into my eyes
pointing your finger for emphasis
and had told me
Family, that's what's important

Today, I turn on the news to see
a little boy holding his father's hand
shivering in the New York cold

He's walked hundreds of miles
waded through water
overflowing with fear

If you could speak to this boy
Would you tell him your story?
Would you offer your hand?

If we could be together now
Would you tell me why a small boy
could make you feel so afraid?

Gray Copper

Karen Colstrom

![butterfly on milkweed flowers]

Malneirophrenia

One-Act Play
Brian C. Billings

CHARACTERS
>APHRODITE, the goddess of love (in voice only)
>EROS, the god of desire and husband to PSYCHE
>HYPNOS, the god of sleep
>THE ONEIROI, the sons of HYPNOS (all in one body)
>>MORPHEUS, bringer of dreams of humans
>>PHANTASOS, bringer of dreams of the inanimate
>>PHOBETOR, bringer of dreams of animals
>PSYCHE, the most beautiful woman in the world and wife to EROS

TIME AND PLACE
>The action takes place in Hypnos's grotto in Erebos, the place of eternal darkness, deep in the Underworld.

>(Dim, golden light rises to reveal the grotto of HYPNOS. The light spills from six inverted torches bracketed evenly along the US wall. Water diverted from the nearby River Lethe trickles through channels carved in the rough stone. Columns hollowed out with alcoves stretch to the ceiling at either end of the room. Each column contains multiple shelves stuffed with leather-cased scrolls. Three S-shaped lounging couches with grey-and-gold cushions rest at CS, CSR, and CSL. HYPNOS, dressed in a pigeon-grey tunic and ochre sandals, perches on the edge of the CSR couch while perusing an unrolled scroll on his lap. A pot of ink rests to his left, and he taps a bronze stylus absently against the eagle wings that sprout from his head. EROS enters at SL as the epitome of weariness. His normally white tunic is blotched with stains. His wings droop, and HE drags his bow and quiver of arrows behind him. Even the straps securing his sandals to his calves are loose.)

HYPNOS

Late again, Eros. I've been waiting nearly twenty minutes. Wings and weapons at the door, please.

>(EROS drops his bow and quiver to the ground. HE pulls a clasp at his left shoulder, and his wings slide off his shoulders into a fluffy heap. HE shuffles to the CS couch and flops down on his back with a groan.)

EROS

I can't sleep. It's been *months*.

HYPNOS

You were just here last week.

EROS

Well, it's been months in mortal time, and I spend more time there than here.

HYPNOS

I hope you haven't been overexerting yourself.

(HE sets aside the scroll.)

EROS

If only. I don't have the focus for that. There's a man in Thrace who's madly in love with his dinner because I took a bad shot.

HYPNOS

Maybe he'll become an epicurean.

EROS

Optimist.

HYPNOS

A misfire isn't necessarily a mistake. Recall, if you will, the affair of the lizard, the rock, and the arrow. The results have been quite popular.

EROS

I suppose. I'm told there's good eating on a turtle.

HYPNOS

Especially in soup...which is where you seem to find yourself these days.

EROS

Nights, Hypnos. Days I can deal with.

HYPNOS

No improvement at all?

EROS

None.

(HYPNOS reclaims his scroll. HE dips his stylus in the ink and begins taking notes while HE talks.)

HYPNOS

Let's check the symptoms just to be certain. Tossing and turning.

EROS

More like thrashing and rolling. Poseidon could take lessons.

HYPNOS

Delayed reaction time.

EROS

I crashed into Mother's statue over in Athens.

Blurry vision, I assume.

EROS

How else can you fail to see a sculpture forty feet high? I think I knocked an arm off.

HYPNOS

Oh, that happens all the time.

EROS

Tell that to Mother.

HYPNOS

I enjoy my existence, thank you. Lack of appetite?

EROS

I can manage maybe half a cup of ambrosia. Any more than that sits like a stone in my stomach. Mostly I've been having warm nectar before bedtime.

HYPNOS

Snacks aren't meals.

EROS

I'm doing the best I can!

HYPNOS

And there's the last one: irritability. Breathe, Eros.

(EROS takes a breath, holds it for a four-count, and exhales.)

EROS

I can't get her out of my mind, Hypnos.

HYPNOS

By *her* you mean Psyche.

EROS

I need her. She's my wife!

HYPNOS

We've talked about this. She burned you, Eros. Badly.

EROS

I shouldn't have stormed out on her.

HYPNOS

You were hurt.

EROS

I was confused! I woke up with a face full of hot wax, and there she was poking a candle in my eyes. I panicked! I needed to get away!

HYPNOS

So flighty.

EROS

Mother says that, too.

HYPNOS

She also told you Psyche left.

EROS

I would feel that. I would know! I keep thinking I hear her voice …especially at night. I reach out expecting to find her sleeping by my side, but every time there's only air. Someone's taken her. One of the other gods, probably. Maybe Hades. He's done that kind of thing before.

HYPNOS

He wouldn't. He's happy with Persephone.

EROS

Then why can't I find her? She's not in the Heavens. She's nowhere on Earth. I had Charon check the ferry manifest, and she hasn't crossed into the Underworld. I hope you'd say something if you'd seen her.

HYPNOS

I would.

EROS

Then I have to keep looking. We might be dealing with metamorphosis or some kind of sealing. She wouldn't be the first girl trapped in a tree.

HYPNOS

Nor the last, I think, but let's help you find some way to rest before you dig up the countryside.

EROS

I can't afford the delay!

HYPNOS

Yet here you are keeping our usual appointment.

EROS

Out of habit. And …you seem like you care.

HYPNOS

Then trust me when I say that closing your eyes now will help you see better later.

(HE scribbles some final thoughts and traces the Greek symbol for air over the scroll. An echoing chime sounds. HE tests the now-dry ink with a finger and nods with satisfaction. HE rolls up his notes and sets the stylus behind an ear.)

I want to try a different technique. Tell me about your dreams.

EROS

I can't sleep! Remember?

HYPNOS

Even the worst insomniac drops off upon occasion. Call it a microsleep. You wouldn't even register the blackout, but a dream can live in a handful of seconds.

EROS

Then I don't dream.

HYPNOS

More likely you don't remember the dreams.

> (HE calls off SR.)

Morpheus!

> (A young god enters. MORPHEUS' clothes perfectly duplicate HYPNOS's raiment, but his tunic is chalked with abstract shapes. MORPHEUS wears a half-mask with wolf ears and black fur. Two other half-masks hang from a belt at his waist: one framed in small gems and one with hyper-extended black eyes. HE growls when HE spots EROS.)

HYPNOS (CONT.)

Oh. Phobetor. I didn't realize you were dominant. I want to talk to Morpheus. Bring him out, won't you?

> (The young man ducks his head. HE removes his mask, places it on his belt, and puts on the large-eyed mask to become MORPHEUS.)

MORPHEUS

Father. Will you need me long? Phobetor was herding the golden sheep for tonight's counting.

HYPNOS

He can do his woolgathering later. I need your help with a client.

MORPHEUS

Waking or sleeping?

HYPNOS

Waking. Tell me how often Eros has been dreaming.

(MORPHEUS crosses to EROS. MORPHEUS kneels behind the god and places his fingers lightly on EROS's temples. EROS flinches.)

EROS

Cold hands!

MORPHEUS

Small wonder. I dwell at length among the dark recesses of the mind.

EROS

And now I'm terrified.

HYPNOS

You're in good hands.

EROS

But can I get out of them?

HYPNOS

Don't worry. He's harmless, and we only need a moment.

(MORPHEUS releases EROS and rises.)

MORPHEUS

He dreams constantly, Father, but strangely. The same visions rise and fall and return without change.

HYPNOS

No wonder he's exhausted. He's been running a marathon. Can you tell me why?

MORPHEUS

I can sense patterns repeating, but a veil clouds the details.

HYPNOS

You're the god of dreams. There shouldn't be a problem.

MORPHEUS

Agreed. I find the experience...frustrating. I suggest a projection.

HYPNOS

Excellent idea! Find a kylix and bring over some water.

(MORPHEUS crosses to the column at SL and removes a wide-bowled drinking cup from one of the alcoves. EROS jerks upright in alarm.)

EROS

Excuse me! I'm not sure I *want* a projection.

(MORPHEUS moves over to the wall and collects Lethe water in the cup.)

HYPNOS

Perhaps *projection* has the wrong flavor. *Construction* describes the procedure better, I think. Working from sensation, my sons and I will build what we find in your dreams layer by layer. Phantasos will set the scene, Phobetor will populate it, and Morpheus will animate it.

(MORPHEUS returns to EROS's side and offers him the cup.)

Once we can see what's been causing you distress, you can confront it and banish it. Drink the water, please.

EROS

That's water from the Lethe! I want my wits to stay where they are.

HYPNOS

The water's *filtered*, and I was about to bestow a blessing anyway.

(HE traces the Greek symbol for water over the cup. A rippling chime sounds.)

You'll only forget your anxieties. I swear. We can't build a proper construct if you're fussing like a wet sphinx.

    (MORPHEUS presses the cup closer to EROS.)

EROS

I'll be able to sleep afterwards?

HYPNOS

Deeper than Endymion.

MORPHEUS

We think.

HYPNOS

The odds are good.

MORPHEUS

Even at the least.

EROS

Well, why not? Nothing else has helped.

    (HE takes the cup and drinks from it lightly. MORPHEUS takes the cup and places it on the ground near the edge of the couch.)

HYPNOS

Now repeat the mantra I taught you a few weeks ago.

EROS

A grand Greek god gives grace to good Greeks.

HYPNOS

Slower.

EROS

A grand...Greek god gives...grace to good...Greeks.

HYPNOS

Slower!

EROS

A grand...Greek god...gives...grace...to...

    (The torchlight begins pulsing in a slow rhythm. EROS relaxes completely. HE stares into a misty distance. MORPHEUS crosses to him and runs his hands over and around EROS's head.)

MORPHEUS

He lies entranced, Father. Phantasos can begin now.

    (MORPHEUS ducks his head and swaps his mask with the begemmed mask. PHANTASOS moves his arms in a slow, cyclical fashion. Lights dim in the main area even as they rise DSL on a freestanding screen. Mounds of grains and seeds—barley, corn, millet, poppies, and wheat—appear on the screen in projection. A barefooted PSYCHE, clad in an elaborately pinned tunic of purple and yellow, walks out from behind the screen. SHE carries an urn filled with more grains and seeds. SHE looks as weary as EROS. Even so, SHE remains eerily beautiful. PHANTASOS swaps masks to become PHOBETOR, who scratches at the air. Small dots of light appear around PSYCHE's feet. PHOBETOR swaps masks to become MORPHEUS, who forms a triangle with his fingers. The dots of light begin marching. PSYCHE speaks, but EROS provides her voice.)

PSYCHE

Here are the grains and the seeds I have gathered in order to satisfy
What you demand. In this urn are the best from the dunes I have
Piled in the hopes they will please you and finally finish my sifting through
Plants from the harvest. Although I am tired, if you find any fault in the
Gifts that I bring, I will gladly begin with my sifting again. Are you
Pleased with my work, Aphrodite so fair? Does the grist of the crop on the
Ground make you smile? Though I may have been helped by industrious
Ants who were moved by my plight, I was never at rest. They were merely a
Means by which sorting came faster. They guided my hands into mastery.

(Red light flashes angrily. The projected mounds shake and dissolve. PSYCHE flails around in the grip of a small earthquake. APHRODITE's voice sneers at her from offstage.)

APHRODITE

Gather the grains! Your ordeal is not over! Your helpers have ruined you!

(PSYCHE vanishes in a blackout. Lights rise to normal in the main area. ORPHEUS shakes out his fingers as if they've been stung. EROS begins thrashing on the couch. HYPNOS holds him down.)

EROS

Psyche! Psyche!

HYPNOS

Morpheus! More water!

(HYPNOS waves an arm, and the torchlight stops pulsing. MORPHEUS scoops up the kylix and forces a drink past EROS's lips. After a beat, EROS relaxes.)

MORPHEUS

Aphrodite's in his dreams, Father.

(HE sets the cup back on the ground. HYPNOS begins pacing.)

HYPNOS

No, no. Just her voice. She can't push in much more than that. She'd be trespassing on your territory. But Psyche's really there! She's not a construct. Aphrodite's trapped her in her husband's dreams. No wonder he couldn't find her.

MORPHEUS

My realm is preternatural. Should she remain there, her substance will erode.

HYPNOS

That's the point. Aphrodite can kill Psyche and torture her son at the same time ...and nobody would have known if Eros hadn't come in for counseling. Clever.

MORPHEUS

Why torture him?

HYPNOS

For loving Psyche. Keep up, son! Classic overprotectiveness. Or jealousy. Either way, she's a wonderfully nasty mother, isn't she?

MORPHEUS

Eros is helping. The ants arise from sympathetic intuition.

HYPNOS

True, but the dream keeps repeating.

MORPHEUS

Which makes him feel like he's failing her.

HYPNOS

Which means?

MORPHEUS

He can't sleep.

HYPNOS

You make me so proud sometimes! Can you pull Psyche out of there?

MORPHEUS

I'll need to study the dream for cracks.

HYPNOS

Then we should press on. Eros, can you hear me?

EROS

Mother?

HYPNOS

Thankfully not. Use your words, Eros. A grand Greek god...

EROS

...gives grace to good Greeks.

(HYPNOS waves a hand in a circle. The torchlight begins pulsing once more.)

HYPNOS

A greater Greek god...

EROS

...gives grateful Greeks grandeur.

HYPNOS

Again.

(EROS recites, and his words slowly fade out. MORPHEUS swaps masks and becomes
PHANTASOS, who begins conjuring the dream. Lights fade in the main area and rise
on the DSL screen. The projection is now the River Estige's ferocious waterfall. Jagged
rocks stick out of the dark water like spears. PSYCHE, holding a stoppered amphora,
steps out from behind the screen. SHE is drenched. PHANTASOS swaps masks to
become PHOBETOR, who spreads out his fingers and shakes them. The outline of an
eagle appears on one of the rocks. PHOBETOR swaps masks to become MORPHEUS,
who gives the scene life. The eagle-shape begins flapping its wings in a stop-motion
fashion. PSYCHE holds out the amphora and speaks in EROS's voice.)

PSYCHE

Water you wanted, and water I have. My amphora contains more than
What you might want. Though the water descending so swiftly was strong, I was
Brave as I stepped on the slippery stones. With a single misstep I would
Surely have shattered my body and perished at once. It's a blessing an
Eagle was passing and pitied my efforts at catching the drops of the
Estige's flood. On a swoop through the spray he took off with my vessel, and
Then he returned with my amphora filled. He was even so kind as to
Guide me to safety. Without his indulgence I doubt I'd have managed the
Path to the bank. Now my task is complete. You can set me at liberty.

(APHRODITE's voice rises offstage.)

APHRODITE

When will you learn? These assignments are never for others' completion.
Liberty. When have I shackled you? Do as I say and my Eros will
Fly to your side. You agreed that my tasks would provide me with proof that your
Love was sincere. Is a little assurance too much for a mother to
Ask? Will you act on your own? If you won't, then my son should be rid of you.

(PSYCHE turns back to the waterfall in resignation. A spotlight rises on MORPHEUS.
HE cries out and reaches for her.)

MORPHEUS

Psyche, your hand! You are trapped in a vision! Your husband is here with me!
Though you've not heard me before, I am Morpheus, shaper of fantasy.
Hypnos, my father, attends you as well at the height of your misery.

APHRODITE

Silence, you godling! Although you are Lord of the Dreams, my command of the
Bond that evolves out of love is a power you can't dissipate though you
Strike it with force or with words. If you only will wait, she will atrophy.
Silence will reign in your realm, and I swear to depart with alacrity.

MORPHEUS

Psyche, again I appeal! Will you give me your hand? I can… . That is …

(APHRODITE laughs as MORPHEUS fumbles for words. Red light flashes, and
PSYCHE fades from view. MORPHEUS's spotlight falls as the main lighting reasserts
itself. HE snaps his fingers in frustration. HYPNOS draws the Greek symbol for earth

and holds out his hands to either side of the symbol. A cymbal crash erupts and fades.
The torches pulse faster.)

HYPNOS

We need to return! We nearly had her!

MORPHEUS

I'm sorry, Father. Dactylic hexameter is difficult!

(HYPNOS's hands begin to shake.)

HYPNOS

Save the apologia for later. I can't preserve the link for long.

(EROS sits up. HE remains entranced.)

EROS

Give her back, Mother! I'll bring you sparrows and swans! Myrtles and roses!

HYPNOS

He's waking up!

EROS

Your vanity is killing us!

(MORPHEUS scoops the kylix off the floor and splashes the last of the water into
EROS's face. EROS drops to the couch unconscious. MORPHEUS places his brothers'
masks over his own. HE crosses to HYPNOS and spreads out his arms. HE and
HYPNOS make a pushing motion together. Lights drop on them as a harsh spotlight
rises on PSYCHE at DSL. SHE stands in front of the screen, which is blank and dark.
Her clothes are dry, her hair is styled, and SHE wears golden sandals. SHE holds a
small wooden box close to her chest. SHE speaks, but this time SHE uses her own
voice.)

PSYCHE

Over and over I've slaved in your trials believing my labors were
Proving my worth. Now I learn you've misled me and all of my effort was
Fuel for your cruelty. Never again will I heed your commands! You've a
Reckoning coming with ultimate prejudice. Psyche the servant no
Longer obeys you. She brings you instead her own means of escaping.
Here is the box with Persephone's beauty you bade me to beg from the
Queen of the Dead. If I swallow the contents to aid my attraction then
Surely my charms will expand in degree so that even a goddess will
Fail to compare. I dismiss you! My beauty delivers your banishment!

(SHE opens the box and consumes what lies within. SHE drops the box to the ground
and kneels. A furiously bright kaleidoscope of color bathes her. APHRODITE shrieks.
PSYCHE vanishes in a blackout. Lights immediately rise in HYPNOS's chamber. The
torches are still. PSYCHE now kneels directly in front of HYPNOS and MORPHEUS,
who lean upon each other. THEY separate as PSYCHE rises, and HYPNOS guides her to
EROS. MORPHEUS removes his layered masks. HE wobbles and switches into
PHOBETOR to regain some primal strength. HE crosses to PSYCHE's side. SHE sits on
the couch and takes EROS's head in her lap. HE stirs and tries to rise.)

EROS

Found you.

(SHE pulls him back down.)

PSYCHE

You did. Don't leave me again.

EROS

Never!

PSYCHE

Then sleep.

(SHE turns down his eyelids, and HE sleeps.)

Thank you, Hypnos. And thanks to you, too, Morpheus.

(PHOBETOR whines.)

HYPNOS

I'm afraid that's Phobetor. Morpheus couldn't hold on any longer.

PSYCHE

I understand.

(SHE scratches PHOBETOR between the ears.)

Good boy.

(HE pants happily.)

HYPNOS

You two should be safe in the grotto.

PSYCHE

We can deal with Aphrodite.

HYPNOS

Boldly stated, but, actually, you can't. She's hardly Hestia. Besides, she's made this a godly matter now. Let me talk to Zeus. He has his ways of sorting out his daughter. He usually enjoys it.

(HE crosses to the SL entrance.)

Come along, son. We need to find our fancy tunics. And maybe some pears. Hera likes those, doesn't she?

(HYPNOS exits. After another head-scratch from PSYCHE, PHOBETOR follows his father. PSYCHE lies down with her husband. PHOBETOR stops at the exit and becomes PHANTASOS. HE makes the Greek symbol for fire, which prompts a muted whoomp. The torches begin dying out. HE exits. Blackout.)

Fairly Certain

David Sapp

It's snowing
And I am certain
Fairly certain
It will snow again
Settling lightly
Upon the orchard
Just so just so
A whirlwind of white
Unpruned branches
An exquisite chaos
Just beyond
My window for
Nearly thirty years
I have anticipated
A whirlwind of white
Blossoms each spring
But now too weary
Its limbs brittle
Dry old bones
I am certain
Fairly certain
There will be no
Flurry of petals
Only the saw
It's heartrending
But I am certain
(Never absolutely certain)
I'll see snow again

Moody Blues at Sundown

Karen Colstrom

The Quiet Body

Dave Malone

Underneath the January snow
lives the garden. This plot is becoming
by sitting still as if reading a book
in wool-socked feet by the fireplace,
with a whiskey in tumbler,
nut brown and warm.

In the fresh snow drift,
I stop garden side
and put elbows to fence
breathing in the silent nature
of this winter quilt,
blocks of last year's basil,
stumps of tomato plants,
stones to mark the rows.

There's a lot happening here
in the quiet body of the garden,
this old lover readying the soil for roots,
for my selfish and greedy hands,
for my fingers full of seed,
for next year's bounty.

All Under One Sky

One-Act Play
Sherrie Pesta

CHARACTERS

   Hannah (F, mid 20's – mid 30's) ... mom
   Alex (M, mid 20's – mid 30's) ... dad #1
   Julian (M, late 30's – early 40's) ... dad #2
   Bonnie (F, 10-12) ... daughter
    Alan (M, 8-10) ... son

SETTING

   Four Lawn Chairs. Two sit CR, facing DSL; two sit CL, facing DSR. A cooler is placed C, serving as a sort of table. There are bags on either end of the line to hold props.

Scene One

(It's July, 1969, near Cape Canaveral, Florida. HANNA sits in the far SR chair, beside BONNIE, SRC. ALEX sits in the far SL chair, beside ALAN, SLC. The children are dressed in jean shorts with off white t-shirts and tennis shoes or flip flops. The parents reflect late 1960's fashion. Snacks, cameras, perhaps a small radio, may be seen. It's early morning. As lights rise, music might provide context of time.)

ALAN

How long do we have to sit here?

ALEX

Until the rocket launches. It shouldn't be much longer.

BONNIE

You should have brought something to do. *(She draws on a pad or Etch-a-sketch)* Like I did.

HANNAH

(To Alan) You don't want to miss this, sweetie. America is making history today.

ALAN

(Brief pause) But I'm hungry.

BONNIE

You're always hungry.

HANNAH

   (Passing him a pop tart)

   Try not to eat too fast.

                                 ALEX
Is that the last pop tart?

                                HANNAH
Yes. Let him have it. He's growing tall. You're only growing wide.

                                 ALEX
Cheerios?

        (HANNAH shakes 'no').

Bugles?

                                HANNAH
Gone. I promise to make you a hearty lunch.

                                 ALEX
A bologna sandwich. With mayo.

                                HANNAH
If that's what you want.

                                 ALEX
Hand me the coffee thermos, at least.

        (HANNAH does.)

Maybe we should have gotten a sitter.

                                HANNAH
I want to see their faces when the rocket lifts. A mother wants to see their children explore the world.

                                 ALEX
They could have watched it on television. (Pause) Did you bring the camera?

        (She pulls it out and hands it to him.)

Is there film in it?

                                HANNAH
Brand new cannister.

        (She turns to BONNIE)

What are you drawing?

                                BONNIE
(Beaming) The rocket. Isn't it amazing?

                                HANNAH
(Throwing an "I told you so" look at ALEX)

Your drawing is amazing, too, Bonnie. Maybe you'll go to Art School one day.

                            ALAN

I'm HOT.

                            BONNIE

It's Florida. In July. (To Mom) I want to go to the moon one day.

                            ALAN

Girls can't go to the moon.

                            HANNAH

Times are changing. A woman today can do and be anything she wishes.

                            ALEX

Realistically...

                            HANNAH

Anything!

                            ALAN

Dad went to college! Didn't you, Dad.

                            ALEX

(Proudly) I certainly did! Two years at Rollins College studying Business. That's why I'm a successful shop manager today.

                            BONNIE

Did you go to college, mom?

                            HANNAH

I wanted to. I wanted to study education, be a teacher.

                            BONNIE

Why didn't you?

                            HANNAH

My father didn't see the point in a woman going to college.

                            ALEX

(To Bonnie) Your mom didn't need a degree. We became engaged in high school. Her father knew I would take care of her.

        (Silence.)

                            BONNIE

Well, I'm going to college.

                            HANNAH

Of course, you are.

                            ALEX

We'll see when the time comes.

ALAN
(Conveniently interrupting the awkward silence.)

Dad, do you think the astronauts will meet someone on the moon?

BONNIE
(Laughing) Who? A little green man? I suppose you also think the moon is made of cheese.

ALAN
Ooh! Cheese!

ALEX
I doubt there are people...or little green men...on the moon, Alan. But, even if there are, *our MEN* will plant the American flag on the moon's surface and claim it for our beautiful country, home of the free.

(HANNAH is trying to get reception on radio.)

HANNAH
Alex, SHUSH! The countdown!

(ALEX does not like being shushed. They stare at sky in silence. HANNAH may hand binoculars to kids.)

ALEX
Blast off!

BONNIE
It's going SO HIGH!

ALAN
(Eyes still looking upwards)

I need to go to the bathroom.

BONNIE
I wonder if any of the astronauts are afraid of heights.

ALAN
Men are not afraid of anything.

BONNIE
(To Mom) Will they be gone long? I feel bad for the moms and children left behind.

ALAN
I want to take a picture.

BONNIE
You'd break the camera.

(A few more moments of silence before they look down.)

HANNAH
I'm breathless.

                                    ALEX
That was a fine, patriotic sight.

                                    ALAN
Can we go now?

                                    ALEX
        (Standing, to Alan)

Come on, son. Let's find you a bathroom while the girls pack up.

        (Lights down.)

                                Scene Two

        (It's March, 1997, near Phoenix, Arizona. HANNAH has made a slight costume change
        to reflect time and has moved into SRC chair. BONNIE has moved out to SR. She wears
        a sweater, cap, tennis shoes. ALAN has moved to SL chair, wearing a sweatshirt, cap,
        tennis shoes. JULIAN, in attire reflecting the late 1990s, has replaced ALEX, in SLC
        chair. He has an expensive camera with tripod, etc. It's evening, between 9 and 10 PM.
        Several pairs of binoculars may still be out. Remains of a picnic are on cooler. As lights
        gradually rise, music might help set mood / time.)

                                    ALAN
Why do we have to sit here? The campground has a pool.

                                    HANNAH
It's too cold to swim at night, Alan. Maybe if it warms up tomorrow... .

                                    BONNIE
You should have brought something to do.

        (She has a portable cassette player and headphones)

I did.
                                    JULIAN
We've been hiking all day, little man. Aren't you exhausted? And don't forget why we came to
Arizona.

                                    ALAN
To see little *green* men.

                                    JULIAN
UFO's. Unidentified Flying Objects. This is supposed to be the place to see them. Aren't you
curious?

                                    ALAN
I'm hungry.

                                    BONNIE
You're always hungry.

(HANNAH offers string cheese.)

ALAN

And thirsty! It's so dry out here.

(JULIAN gives him a juice box.)

BONNIE

It's Arizona.

HANNAH

Do you have the fliers, Julian? I'm not sure what I'm looking for.

JULIAN
(Handing her a colorful brochure)
Could be anything out of the ordinary. A saucer-like shape. Flashing lights. The Park Ranger said he has seen countless unexplained occurrences.

BONNIE

I want to be a Park Ranger one day. It's so peaceful and quiet out here.

(She bobs to her music.)

HANNAH

How can you tell, dear? Cut that music down before you harm your ears.

ALAN

Girls can't be Park Rangers. Only MEN are strong enough to fight off a bear or coyote.

JULIAN
(Pointing up the trail)

Actually, there are two female Park Rangers just ahead. Women can do and be anything they wish to.

ALAN

I suppose.

BONNIE

Look at Mom! She's a successful Engineer.

JULIAN
(With a tad of jealousy?)

That's right. An MIT graduate, surpassing most men in the field.

HANNAH
(Overcompensating) No more successful than my award-winning, photojournalist, husband!

JULIAN
I have just been lucky. Been at the right places at the right time. I could not afford university tuition.

HANNAH

Yet look what you have done with natural talent and determination! Your photos are nationally syndicated!

JULIAN

Maybe I'll be in the right place at the right time today, too.

(Switching conversation to son)

What do you think an alien looks like, Alan? I bet they have six arms and four eyes. What a photo shoot that could be!

BONNIE

They probably look a lot like us. ... Though maybe less fashionable.

ALAN

Maybe we should save some of the string cheese. So, they can eat IT. Instead of US.

(Pause. Laughter)

I need to go to the bathroom.

HANNAH

If you leave the safety of our circle, aren't you afraid an alien might abduct you?

ALAN

I'm not afraid of anything. I'd *like* to ride in a spaceship. See an alien planet.

BONNIE

Mom, do scientists believe in aliens?

HANNAH

Well.... Belief is a personal...

BONNIE

... I don't want to be abducted. I don't want to leave you behind, Mom! Dad, wouldn't you feel sad?

ALAN

They'd still have me.

BONNIE

Sad.

(Lights suddenly flash across the stage, and theyall look towards the sky. Gasps. Long Pause. Then they begin to whisper to one another.

HANNAH

I didn't *believe*... we would really see....

JULIAN

(Shooting pictures wildly with a professional camera)

... I don't know what that is ...

                                    HANNAH
Does that look like a 'v'?

                                     ALAN
IT'S A SHIP!

                                    BONNIE
With flashing lights!

                                     ALAN
Take a picture of me with it!

                                    BONNIE
You'd break the camera.

          (They stare. Pause. They look down.)

                                    JULIAN
Wow. I was not expecting that.

                                    HANNAH
          (Standing. To ALAN)

Come on, sweetheart.

          (She snatches camera from JULIAN)

I'll take a picture of you on the edge of that field while your sister and dad start to pack up.

                                     ALAN
Can I take a picture myself?

                                    HANNAH
          (Looking at JULIAN, she hands expensive camera to son)

Sure.

                                     ALAN
          (Holding camera recklessly, Alan runs off)

Yea!

          (HANNAH follows as Lights go down.)

                                Scene Three

(It's January, 2023, on the deck of an Alaskan Cruise Ship. BONNIE and ALAN return to C chairs. They are now covered in blankets. They wear coats, hats, gloves. JULIAN has moved to SL chair and is similarly covered for the cold weather. ALEX has replaced HANNAH in SR chair, also dressed warmly, and covered with a blanket. All have cameras and mugs of hot chocolate. It's around midnight. For a moment, they all stare silently into the sky. ALEX and JULIAN are obviously delighted. BONNIE and ALAN have begun to get bored and tired. As lights rise, music might indicate time and place.)

BONNIE

How long do we have to sit quietly. It's been hours.

JULIAN

It's been twenty minutes. Twenty glorious minutes!

ALAN

You should have brought something to do.

(Pulls out a Gameboy)

Like I did.

(Begins to play.)

ALEX

Put that away! We are here to experience the Northern Lights, together! Not play a video game.

ALAN

(Alan grumpily puts it away. Pause.)

I'm hungry.

BONNIE

You're always hungry. The buffet is closed. They need time to restock because of you.

ALAN

And I'm FREEZING.

BONNIE

It's Alaska. In January.

(Starting to agree with ALAN.)

And we're sitting on a boat deck, surrounded by ICE. At MIDNIGHT!

JULIAN

(To ALEX) Perhaps it is time for the kids to retire.

ALEX

And miss this once-in-a-lifetime opportunity?

ALAN

I'm not a kid.

ALEX

SEE! They can handle a little cold for just a bit longer.

(To BONNIE and ALAN)

Where are the polaroids I bought you? Maybe you'll catch a whale in your photo. Or a polar bear.

JULIAN

In the dark?

> (ALEX shushes him)

BONNIE

I want to *save* the Polar Bears one day.

JULIAN

Admirable!

ALAN

One 'girl' can't save an entire species.

JULIAN

One 'GIRL' can change the world!

> (Silent pause as they continue to watch. BONNIE and ALAN take pictures with their polaroids.)

ALAN

What are the lights? They look like fire.

ALEX

Ask your father. He's the one with the Doctorate in Mythology.

BONNIE

They look like they are dancing. Maybe the stars are dancing!

JULIAN

According to myth, the Aurora Borealis is a visualization of ancestral *spirits* dancing near earth.

BONNIE

I don't like spirits. ...Are they evil? ... They look so pretty.

JULIAN

Ask your father. He has the Doctorate in Religion.

ALEX

They are said to be the spirits of family members. I don't *believe* they are evil.

BONNIE

Spirits who don't want to leave? That is sad.

ALEX

Or spirits watching over us. Which can be comforting.

JULIAN

> (About ALEX as well as the stars)

Beautiful.

BONNIE

When Alan and I are older, do we have to get Doctorates, too?

                        JULIAN

Only if you wish to.

                        ALAN

Do we HAVE to go to college at all?

                  ALEX and JULIAN

YES!

                        ALEX

At least get a Bachelor's. The world has become a competitive place.

                        JULIAN

A Master's wouldn't hurt.

                        ALAN

(After a groan) I need to go to the bathroom.

                        JULIAN

(Ignoring him) There is another story, a Finnish tale about the lights. They call them 'fox fires', and claim they are started by a Firefox whose tail flings sparks when he runs.

                        ALAN

I like that story! I told you they look like a fire.

        (ALAN cuddles deep into his blanket to fall asleep.)

                        BONNIE

I like the fox better than dead people, too. Maybe he dances while he runs.

        (She cuddles in to sleep, too.)

                        ALEX

Shouldn't we tell them the truth, the scientific causes of the lights?

                        JULIAN

They have plenty of time for truths. Let them enjoy fantasy for a while longer.

                        ALEX

Marrying you remains the best decision I have ever made.

                        JULIAN

You mean besides adopting those two?

                        ALEX

Naturally.

                        JULIAN

Ours is a stars-in-the-sky, kind of story.

        (JULIAN and ALEX stare at the sky.)

        (Lights go down.)

Snow Home

Dave Malone

Red-tailed hawk puffs up
on the utility pole
in the January freeze.

We lock eyes, turn beaks,
then I tromp
through snowdrifts

en route to the far end
of the yard to build a home.
I fashion heavy bricks

from Mother's baking pans
I've stolen though she'll not notice.
I pluck out perfect blocks

with Father's slide rule
he'll never use again.
When I've got the dome completed,

it's time to bring in the sleeping bag
and the neighbor's shell of a dog.
Here we sleep through the afternoon

while the wind hugs our snow home,
and the raptor takes a field mouse
against a gentle whooshing of sleet.

Prairie Palomino

Karen Colstrom

Anxiety

Craig Kirchner

She apologized, all the time, all her life,
she was sorry, but not out loud,
a state of mind that was tiring.
There was no misfortune or distress,
she hadn't thrown anyone in front of a train,
or under a bus but was culpable.

She felt worthy of liable, by default,
didn't say it, she *was* it.
Sorrow darkened the eyes, the soul,
it slowed down alternatives,
conversation, sex, happiness,
any of the pleasures.

Momentarily she could shake it,
have a drink, reflect,
chill out, get something done,
but it resurfaced with the first
bad thought, the first coveting,
lying, lusting - all the basics.

She hadn't done it, or thought it,
yet was building regret,
like worrying about a flat tire,
while you're putting it in drive.
Confession, saying it out loud seemed
like a shell game for suckers.

She had compartmentalized carefully,
built an immunity of walls
to all past grief,
now only needing to be very still,
walk backwards by virtue of doors
she'd already been through.

Lost

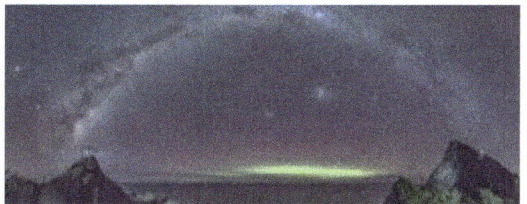

Sherrie Pesta

This One Act is comprised of three scenes. The staging should be simple, symbolic.

CHARACTERS *(In Order of Appearance)*
       ELDERLY MAN (M, 65+)
       YOUNG MAN (M, 20-25)
       YOUNG LADY (F, 19-25)
       YOUNG GIRL (F, 8-10)
       WOMAN (F, 35-45)
       EMT (E)
       DISGRUNTLED (M, 25-35)
       SARCASTIC (F, 25-35)
       BEWILDERED (M, 25-35)
       CUNNING (E, 40-55)

SCENE ONE: In a Park

(A Saturday morning. One bench sits UC. When lights rise, an ELDERLY MAN slumps on the bench, his eyes closed. There's a stack of 'Lost Cat' fliers beside him. He has stuck one of the fliers to the arm of the bench, where the audience can see it.)

(YOUNG MAN enters SR, running to catch a ball. He exits SL after it. YOUNG LADY and YOUNG GIRL enter SR.)

YOUNG LADY

I know what you're doing.

YOUNG GIRL

I doubt it.

YOUNG LADY

Quit making him chase that ball! He's not a dog.

YOUNG GIRL

A dog would be more fun.

YOUNG LADY

Please, don't ruin this for me.

YOUNG GIRL

You said we'd go shopping today.

> YOUNG LADY

We can go tomorrow. We have the whole weekend.

> YOUNG GIRL

But Lavender Bear goes on sale *today*.

> (Sees ELDERLY MAN on bench and points.)

Who's that?

> YOUNG LADY

> (Turns, startled)

My god! Is he asleep?

> (GIRL crosses to MAN and extends hand.)

Don't touch him!

> (YOUNG MAN enters SL with ball.)

> YOUNG MAN

Good throw, kid!

> (Seeing her over the ELDERLY MAN)

Is that man dead?

> (YOUNG GIRL shrieks and YOUNG LADY pulls her in. YOUNG MAN drops ball and crosses UC.)

> YOUNG LADY

Hold something over his face. See if he's breathing.

> (YOUNG MAN wiggles a flier out from pile and holds it in front of ELDERLY MAN's face. Nothing. YOUNG GIRL reads flier.)

> YOUNG GIRL

"Lost Cat"!

> (She takes the flier from YOUNG MAN.)

That's so sad. He must be looking for her.

> YOUNG MAN

Or was.

> (YOUNG MAN whispers.)

Not sure he's breathing.

> (Pause)

Should we call the police?

YOUNG LADY

(Whispering)

That could take all day. They'll question us! We're not supposed to be in a park. I'll get fired!

YOUNG MAN

Calm down.

YOUNG LADY

I should not be here with you. I should have taken her shopping like I promised.

YOUNG GIRL

(Having heard the whispering)

That's what I said.

YOUNG MAN

(Speaking full voice)

I can't just leave this man here.

(Pause. No response.)

You two can leave.

(YOUNG LADY begins to pull YOUNG GIRL out SR. YOUNG GIRL breaks free and returns to bench.)

YOUNG GIRL

(Scooping up a stack of fliers)

We should put up some of his fliers.

YOUNG LADY

If he's (gesturing weakly towards Elderly Man) ... dead..., he's not going to miss a cat.

(YOUNG GIRL scowls at YOUNG LADY, who continues.)

And...if we find the cat...with him being...dead...what then?

YOUNG GIRL

I keep it!

(She runs off SR.)

YOUNG LADY

I am so fired.

(She exits SR.)

YOUNG MAN
(Dialing cell phone)

Yes, I...there's an emergency... . I'm...in Seven Hills Park. ...Near the soccer fields.... There's an Elderly Man on a bench... . What? No, he doesn't appear hurt. ...But he doesn't seem alive either. ...I said alive. I mean... mybe *not* alive?

WOMAN
(Entering SR in a hurry and seeing ELDERLY MAN)

Dad! Thank goodness.

    (She hurries over and hugs him. He slouches over onto bench.)

Oh, no.

YOUNG MAN
(Continuing into phone)

...Probably dead. You should send someone. ... Near the 4th street entrance.

    (Having pushed ELDERLY MAN back up, WOMAN sits. She holds MAN while searching purse. YOUNG MAN hangs up.)

WOMAN
He's not dead. He's diabetic.

    (She finds a shot and shoves it into leg.)

ELDERLY MAN
(Fluttering eyes towards Woman)

Maggie? .... Maggie ....

WOMAN
(Wrapping an arm around his shoulders).

Sshh...

    (He sinks into her, eyes closed again, as she speaks softly to him.)

Quit wandering off alone. You worry me.

YOUNG MAN
Your name is Maggie?

WOMAN
(Without looking up from ELDERLY MAN) No.

YOUNG MAN

(Pause) The cat then.

(She looks at him confused.)

The flier. He's looking for his cat.

WOMAN

The cat ... *is* dead. (Pause) Died over a year ago.

YOUNG MAN

He doesn't know?

WOMAN

Alzheimer's. ...

YOUNG MAN

Alzheimer's *and* Diabetes?

WOMAN

Getting old sucks. ...

(Sounds of an ambulance arriving)

Did I hear you call 9-1-1?

YOUNG MAN

Yes?

WOMAN

I can't afford another ambulance. Help me get him to my car.

YOUNG MAN

(Backing up)

I don't know....

WOMAN

Fine. I'll do it myself.

(She shifts ELDERLY MAN down and talks to him.)

Right back.

(She exits SL.)

YOUNG MAN

WHERE ARE YOU ...?

(He paces nervously. He decides to cross UC and examine ELDERLY MAN. He lifts ELDERLY MAN and leans him back up on bench. EMT enters SL.)

EMT

Avoid touching the patient, please!

(YOUNG MAN releases and the ELDERLY MAN slides down face first. EMT rushes to bench.)

EMT

Are you this man's son?

(YOUNG MAN shakes head 'no'.)

Grandson?

(YOUNG MAN shakes head 'no'.)

Then who...?

YOUNG MAN

... I called 9-1-1.

EMT

So, you found him.

(YOUNG MAN is struck by the words.)

Alone?

YOUNG MAN

No... I was with a ... friend ... and her ...

EMT

Not you. Him. Was HE alone?

(WOMAN enters SR with a cane. Stops out of sight; motions to YOUNG MAN to keep her out of it.)

YOUNG MAN

No ... I mean ... Yes? ... I ... cannot say ... that I saw someone *with* him.

(As the EMT stares, ELDERLY MAN wakes.)

ELDERLY MAN

(To EMT) Who the HELL are you? (Grabbing up fliers*)* MAGGIE?

YOUNG MAN

He seems fine now. Maybe you could just let him go home.

EMT

With whom? ... Who's Maggie? ... (Pause.) You're not related to him? (Pause) ... Listen, we need to check him out. If he's 'fine,' and *someone* wants to take him home...we will consider releasing him into a *relative's* custody.

EMT guides ELDERLY MAN off SL. WOMAN enters SR and storms up to YOUNG MAN.)

WOMAN

Why do you have to be involved? You don't have your own problems to solve?

YOUNG MAN

I thought you didn't want to pay for an ambulance.

WOMAN

(Pause. Almost tearful) I'm *not* a terrible daughter.

YOUNG MAN

Of course not. ... I didn't say you were. (Pause) It must be really ... difficult to ...

WOMAN

(Exiting SL hurriedly) Thank you. DAD! Wait!

YOUNG GIRL

(Entering SR) Where's the old guy?

YOUNG MAN

Gone.

YOUNG GIRL

Lost?

YOUNG MAN

You might say that.

YOUNG GIRL

We got lost, too!

YOUNG MAN

What do you mean? Where's ....?

YOUNG LADY

(Entering SR, exhausted) We got confused putting up fliers in these woods.

YOUNG GIRL

(Full of happy energy*)* Then we heard an ambulance!

> (YOUNG MAN points out SL and YOUNG GIRL runs off. YOUNG LADY starts to exit, but YOUNG MAN stops her.)

YOUNG MAN

Let her go. You can see her from here.

YOUNG LADY

She could get hurt.

YOUNG MAN

What could happen with an EMT standing right beside her?

> (He reaches for one of her hands.)

YOUNG LADY
(Slipping past him to cross to the remaining fliers on the ground)

Help me throw these away. I'm not hanging any more fliers today.

YOUNG MAN
(Taking the fliers from her gently and holding her hand)

You don't have to. The cat's not lost.

YOUNG LADY

Thank goodness!

YOUNG MAN

The cat's dead.

YOUNG LADY
(Overwhelmed) NO! (Panicking) Not the man, too?

YOUNG MAN

Might as well be.

YOUNG LADY
(Pause. Looking pale and exhausted.)

I feel so … helpless.

YOUNG MAN
(Pause. He gazes at her.)

Let's start over. Go somewhere less … whatever this is. … Tomorrow?

YOUNG LADY
(Tired) I will be with munchkin all day. If I disappear, try searching Build-a-Bear.

YOUNG MAN
Next Saturday, then. Next Saturday *Night*. We could see a movie.

YOUNG LADY
(Pause) Sure.

(They begin walking to exit SL.)

What could go wrong?

(Lights down.)

Scene Two: In a Break Room
(Monday. It's lunch hour in a chain store break room. Several aluminum chairs surround a card table, DSR/DC. An easel holds a bulletin board, DL. On the board hang a work duty schedule, sign-up sheets for intramural teams, and a "Lost Cat" flier. A small table UC holds a coffee pot and cups. When lights rise, DISGRUNTLED and SARCASTIC are unpacking their lunches. They wear sweaters.)

DISGRUNTLED

That's the second store lock-down in a week. If parents just kept an eye on their children, they wouldn't get lost.

SARCASTIC

Now why blame the parents? No one is perfect. So, they let their little ones play tag through the lingerie or hide-and-seek around the lawnmowers. How should they know the dangers involved?

DISGRUNTLED

I'm not here to babysit someone else's poor decision. (Counting out chips). They come in here with not one…not two… but a minivan full. They're not likely to notice at first if a single toddler (eats a chip) goes missing.

> (BEWILDERED enters breakroom. Looks around. He wears a tie and a Manager pin. Heads to coffee.)

SARCASTIC

Speaking of lost….

> (BEWILDERED wanders to their table and sits.)

DISGRUNTLED

The manager's break room is down the hall two doors.

BEWILDERED

(Without moving) Yes.

SARCASTIC

I could draw you a map.

BEWILDERED

No need. I prefer it here.

DISGRUNTLED

Sure. Why choose a newly remodeled lounge with baskets of fresh fruit and a cappuccino machine when you can have all…this.

SARCASTIC

(Admiring DISGRUNTLED) Wow! I'm rubbing off on you.

BEWILDERED

Have you ever stopped and wondered…, "What am I doing with my life? How did I get here?"

DISGRUNTLED and SARCASTIC

Every Morning.	Every Second.
With every dismal Customer.	With every whining Clown.

Why do you ask?

BEWILDERED

(Standing and crossing to easel board.)

I thought this job would be fun. Talking with people … who shop. … I like talking … and shopping.

DISGRUNTLED and SARCASTIC
Uh-huh.

BEWILDERED

But it's boring. Tedious.

DISGRUNTLED

I've been working here over six years. Key word: WORK, *not* 'Fun'.

SARCASTIC

(To DISGRUNTLED) But, my friend, you're a clerk. WE are lowly servants to the masses. THIS man is a MANAGER! Surely, he can expect more FUN out of his time here than we can.

BEWILDERED

Wouldn't you think so! It's all spread sheets, and phone calls. And now I've been put in charge of ...

(Looks around before saying in a loud whisper)

... layoffs!

DISGRUNTLED

Layoffs?

BEWILDERED

Something about making the budget tighter .... Releasing 20%, the 'dead weight'.

(He looks at the schedules posted on the board.)

I guess I could just randomly pick names.

SARCASTIC

(Standing angrily) And I could just randomly poison a cappuccino machine!

(DISGRUNTLED pulls on SARCASTIC's sweater.)

DISGRUNTLED

Perhaps the two of us could aid you in some way? We could ... share insider secrets.

SARCASTIC

Of course! We know all the gossip. From who drinks in the dressing rooms to who takes one piece out of every puzzle box just for kicks.

DISGRUNTLED

(Pointing to a name on the sign in sheet)

Thomas here totes his teacup poodle around in a fanny pack while stocking groceries.

BEWILDERED

Is that hygienic?

SARCASTIC

(Pointing to another name)

And Bethany. She's supposed to be selling baby clothes, so why is she always circling through Cosmetics?

BEWILDERED

She probably gets turned around. It's understandable in a store this enormous.

SARCASTIC

Let's just say someone should do a surprise inventory of the nail polish aisle.

BEWILDERED

(It takes a moment to register.)

One of our employees is a thief?

SARCASTIC

You said it, not me.

CUNNING

(Entering unnoticed) There you are! Did you mistake .... Is it *freezing* in this cubicle?

DISGRUNTLED and SARCASTIC
Always.

CUNNING

(Ignoring them. To BEWILDERED)

What are you doing in here?

BEWILDERED

Talking with these two ....

CUNNING

Interviewing the employees. Fascinating approach.

BEWILDERED

I've been thinking, sir....

CUNNING

That's not what we pay you for.

BEWILDERED

That's just it. What is my purpose here? I'm not feeling I ... fit in.

CUNNING

But you CAN fit in. Here at Winkles, we like to think of ourselves as one big happy TEAM. Us against the world – against our major competitors anyway.

(Pointing to the intramural sign-up sheets, CUNNING continues.)

Can we count on you to help BEAT the competition?

                    BEWILDERED
You want me to join the ...

           (squinting at what Cunning seems to be pointing at)

Pickleball team?

                    CUNNING
What sport are you best at? We need WINNERS!

                    BEWILDERED
I suppose ... baseball?

                    CUNNING
Wonderful!

                    DISGRUNTLED
           (Packing up lunch and standing)

I best get back to finding kidnapped children.

                    CUNNING
It just so happens our intramural Softball team needs a shortstop.

                    BEWILDERED
I was a shortstop on my minor league baseball team, the Wasps! What a crazy coincidence!

                    SARCASTIC
Shocking.

                    CUNNING
You start next Saturday. A winning season could mean a promotion for ALL!

           (DISGRUNTLED and SARCASTIC stop, hearing a glimmer of hope.)

All *Players*, that is.

                    SARCASTIC
           (Standing to exit with DISGRUNTLED.)

While I'm allowed to work double shifts through the games, no doubt.

           (Cunning looks at SARCASTIC. She pivots.)

Yay!

                    CUNNING
           (Eyes on SARCASTIC and DISGRUNTLED, to BEWILDERED.)

Have you started that Layoff list?

           SARCASTIC   DISGRUNTLED
             Gotta fly!   Customers waiting!

(They rush towards the exit.)

                        CUNNING
(See's "Lost Cat" poster). What's this doing on the employee board?

                        DISGRUNTLED
A young girl brought it in. Hoped someone might see the cat.

                        CUNNING
(Ripping it down) If the girl comes back, sell her a stuffed one.

        (Lights down.)

                Scene 3: At the Movies

Next Saturday Night, in the Lobby of a Movie Complex. Off SR is Entrance and
Concessions. UR is the frame of a door with a curtain pulled aside – the entrance to
Theater I, showing an R-rated movie. UL is another door frame with a curtain pulled
aside – entrance to Theater II, showing a G-rated movie. SL exits to the bathrooms. As
lights rise, DISGRUNTLED and SARCASTIC stand C wearing movie uniforms.

                        DISGRUNTLED
I can't believe he sacked me!

                        SARCASTIC
I can.

                        DISGRUNTLED
At least he sacked you, too.

                        SARCASTIC
Harder to believe. I'm such a charmer.

                        DISGRUNTLED
Back to minimum wage. How am I to keep up my lifestyle working 20 hours a week in a
teenager's job?

                        SARCASTIC
Fair concern. Fast food prices are on the rise.

                        DISGRUNTLED
I suppose you shop organic.

                        SARCASTIC
Only for my kitten, Zeus. I can exist on canned peas and smoothies myself.

        (WOMAN and ELDERLY MAN enter SR. Cross C.)

                        ELDERLY MAN
What movie are we seeing?

                        WOMAN
I just told you. We're seeing an animated film. *The Forest Guides.*

ELDERLY MAN

Sounds boring.

DISGRUNTLED

(Tearing tickets and pointing UL) *The Forest Guides* will be in Theater II. Watch your step.

ELDERLY MAN

What's playing in Theater I?

SARCASTIC

Evil Lurks Around the Corner

WOMAN

The title alone gives me shivers.

ELDERLY MAN

Doesn't sound boring at least.

WOMAN

(Dragging him UL) Come on, old man. You'll be the death of me.

(WOMAN and ELDERLY MAN exit UL, to Movie II.)

SARCASTIC

Best not tempt fate.

(CUNNING enters SR with a large drink. Crosses C.)

SARCASTIC

(Tearing his tickets with a glare) *Evil Lurks Around the Corner* in Theater I.

CUNNING

There's something lurking … around a corner?

DISGRUNTLED

(Impatiently and angrily pointing UR) Your MOVIE, Evil. Lurks. Around. The. Corner. is *playing* in Theater I.

CUNNING

Ah! (Starts to exit but stops and stares.) You two look familiar. (Pause) No. Never mind. (Exits UR).

(BEWILDERED and YOUNG GIRL enter SR. Cross C. She has candy and a Lavender Bear.)

BEWILDERED

(Naively) Hey! I didn't see you guys at the game today! I looked for you in the bleachers, but there were so many faces yours could easily have been lost in the crowd.

DISGRUNTLED

(Flatly) Cheered on by the masses, were you?

YOUNG GIRL

Dad was a Hero! He won the game for Winkles.

SARCASTIC

(Shortly) No doubt.

      (YOUNG GIRL crosses L. BEWILDERED watches her. She hangs a Cat Flier near the bathrooms.)

BEWILDERED

(Turning back to hand over tickets) This a side gig? Seems fun. You probably get free movies, too.

DISGRUNTLED

Sure.

      (BEWILDERED has turned attention back to GIRL and doesn't hear.)

SARCASTIC

He's unaware of our circumstances.

DISGRUNTLED

Improbable.

BEWILDERED

(Returning focus to take tickets back) What is?

DISGRUNTLED

Cunning sacked me.

SARCASTIC

He fired us BOTH. And about three other clerks. Don't say you didn't know.

BEWILDERED

(Taken aback) I didn't! Yes, I give him a Layoff list. But neither of your names was on it.

DISGRUNTLED

Sure.

SARCASTIC

And our names are ...?

BEWILDERED

Listen. There's nothing to be done tonight. But I promise to straighten out this mess first thing Monday morning.

      (He waves to YOUNG GIRL)

Come on, baby. (They exit UL.)

DISGRUNTLED

Can we trust him?

SARCASTIC

Friend, I can't even trust you.

>   (YOUNG MAN and YOUNG LADY enter SR. YOUNG MAN crosses C. YOUNG LADY crosses to exit SL, bathrooms.)

YOUNG LADY

Go ahead in. Pick out seats.

YOUNG MAN

I'll wait here.

YOUNG LADY

Fine. I'll hurry. (She exits)

YOUNG MAN
(To DISGRUNTLED and SARCASTIC as he hands tickets)

Has either of you seen *Evil Lurks Around the Corner*?

SARCASTIC

Not technically.

DISGRUNTLED

Though we have seen Evil enter that door.

>   (YOUNG MAN pauses, confused.)

YOUNG MAN

I hope I chose the right movie, that's all. Scary enough to make her cuddle in, but not so scary she gets tearful and wants to vanish.

DISGRUNTLED

The Forest Guardians is playing in Theater II. That sounds mildly scary to me.

YOUNG MAN

Isn't that animated? I'm hoping for romance not cuteness.

>   (DISGRUNTLED shrugs)

Maybe I'll just reread the movie posters. (He exits SR.)

>   (WOMAN and ELDERLY MAN enter UL.)

ELDERLY MAN

I am going to the bathroom BY MYSELF. (She holds cane out.) And WITHOUT that RIDICULOUS STICK!

WOMAN

Fine. But don't linger. If you're not back in your seat in 5 minutes, I'm coming after you.

>   (ELDERLY MAN crosses to exit SL. WOMAN exits UL.)

DISGRUNTLED

Speaking of lurking.

SARCASTIC

Please. If I get so old that people worry I can't go to the bathroom on my own ... just end it.

(EMT enters SR in time to hear her. Crosses C.)

EMT
(Handing SARCASTIC ticket and a pamphlet)

There's a Hot Line # on there to call if you ever want to talk with someone.

(YOUNG MAN reenters SR. Stops DR.)

DISGRUNTLED
(Amusedly pointing UR as SARCASTIC violently tears ticket)

Your movie is playing in Theater I.

(EMT exits UR. YOUNG LADY enters SL. Meets YOUNG MAN DC.)

YOUNG LADY

I hope this movie is not TOO scary. (They cross to exit UR.) Or sad. I hate sad movies.

(DISGRUNTLED and SARCASTIC each cross US to close curtains over doors. They face US. Sounds/Music can be heard from theatres. ELDERLY MAN enters SL. Sees Cat Flier. Takes it. Crosses to exit SR. DISGRUNTLED and SARCASTIC return C.)

DISGRUNTLED

Finally. Peace and ...
SARCASTIC
(As Sounds from movies increase)

... NOT Quiet.

(YOUNG MAN enters UR and crosses to exit SR.)

SARCASTIC

Don Juan on a Raisinets Quest.

(YOUNG GIRL enters UL and crosses to exit SL.)

DISGRUNTLED

Brutus's daughter. ... You never told me he had a daughter.

SARCASTIC

I just met the man! We aren't Instagram chums!

(WOMAN enters from UL and crosses C.)

WOMAN
(To them collectively.) Have you seen my father?

DISGRUNTLED and SARCASTIC
The old man? Didn't he go to the bathroom?
I saw him go into the bathroom earlier. I don't remember seeing him come out.

WOMAN
(Stopping them and pointing to DISGRUNTLED)

You. Please go into the Men's room and look for him.

(DISGRUNTLED exits SL. Awkward silence as WOMAN and SARCASTIC stare after. YOUNG MAN returns from SR with snacks. He crosses C to stand beside SARCASTIC and stare off, too.)

YOUNG MAN
What are you looking at?

SARCASTIC
(Jumping with a small shriek) The entrance to the bathrooms. This Woman's father may be lost.

YOUNG MAN
In the bathrooms? (Realizing, to WOMAN) The Woman from the Park! That old man is lost AGAIN?

WOMAN
Probably.

SARCASTIC
Maybe he's in Theater I. Why don't you two go look. I will wait here in case he's found in the bathroom.

YOUNG MAN
(Hesitant to get involved) Okay.

(YOUNG MAN exits UR. WOMAN follows him. YOUNG GIRL enters SL. Notices that flier is gone.)

YOUNG GIRL
(To SARCASTIC) I put a "Lost Cat" flier up here. Did you take it down?

SARCASTIC
No. But I should have. You can't just put fliers up anywhere you want to.

YOUNG GIRL
Did you see who did?

SARCASTIC
I don't spy...

(YOUNG GIRL rushes C to grab SARCASTIC.)

YOUNG GIRL
Come on!

YOUNG GIRL exits SR, pulling SARCASTIC with her. BEWILDERED enters UL and CUNNING enters UR. They cross C.

CUNNING

My Winner! That was some game this afternoon! Can't thank you enough. Buy you an ICEE?

BEWILDERED

That's alright. I'm just looking for my daughter.

CUNNING

How old?

BEWILDERED

Almost nine.

CUNNING

And she's wandering around alone? What if she gets lost?

BEWILDERED

She just went to the bathroom. She's probably still in there.

(DISGRUNTLED returns SL.)

DISGRUNTLED

If you two are plotting a hostile takeover, you can have this place. I quit!

BEWILDERED

Did you see a young girl in there?

DISGRUNTLED

I was in the MEN's room, looking for a lost MAN. I was NOT in the WOMEN's room, looking for a lost CHILD. Child? Wow. It's as bad here as at Winkles. Maybe we should lock this place down, too.

(WOMAN and EMT enter UR.)

WOMAN

(To DISGRUNTLED) You're back! Did you find him?

DISGRUNTLED

No. I found a disaster in there, which I am NOT cleaning up! But no old man. (Softer) Sorry.

EMT

(To WOMAN) Check the Concessions stand, then the parking lot. Maybe he wandered off to your car. I'll check the Women's room, just in case he got mixed up.

(WOMAN exits SR. CUNNING follows. EMT starts to exit SL. BEWILDERED crosses to EMT.)

BEWILDERED

My daughter may be in there, too. Please look for me?

EMT
Of course. (Shaking head as exits SL) These people could lose their heads... .

(YOUNG MAN and YOUNG LADY enter UR. She waves at BEWILDERED.)

YOUNG LADY
Hi! Where's munchkin? (Overzealously) We had SO much fun stuffing bears last weekend!

BEWILDERED
(In a daze) Yes. Oh, hello. Yes, she's drags that purple stuffie everywhere. Thank you for …. I'm not actually certain where she is right now. She said she was going to the bathroom …

EMT
(Returning from SL) There's no one in either bathroom. I checked both.

YOUNG LADY
She's missing?!

YOUNG MAN
No way. That girl is street savvy.

BEWILDERED
(Crossing towards SR exit) Maybe she smelled popcorn.

(He is stopped at the entrance. CUNNING and WOMAN return SR. SARCASTIC follows with a chair. WOMAN sits. EMT crosses to her.)

EMT
Ma'am, are you alright?

CUNNING
She's having a panic attack. I can empathize. It can be hard to hold so much responsibility.

(YOUNG GIRL and ELDERLY MAN return SR.)

BEWILDERED and WOMAN
YOU DISAPPEARED!

(BEWILDERED rushes to GIRL and sweeps her up. WOMAN rushes to ELDERLY MAN and hugs him. She and EMT guide MAN carefully into chair. SARCASTIC exits SR.)

BEWILDERED
(Still tightly holding YOUNG GIRL) Do you realize how frightened I was?

ELDERLY MAN
(To BEWILDERED) Don't scold the child. It's my doing. She came looking for me.

(SARCASTIC returns with Juice for ELDERLY MAN.)

WOMAN
(To Young Girl) Thank you, sweet girl. How did you know he was missing? Or where to look?

YOUNG GIRL

Someone took the Cat Flier. It had to have been him. I knew he was out there looking for his Cat.

WOMAN

(Resigning to a decision) Then I will have to find her for him, won't I?

YOUNG MAN

But I thought the Cat was …

(YOUNG LADY puts finger on lips to shush him.)

SARCASTIC

I think *finding* his Cat is a wonderful idea.

ELDERLY MAN

(To WOMAN) It's alright, Natalie. My cat, Stormy, is dead.

WOMAN

You remember. …And you called me by *my* name, not *mom's*.

ELDERLY MAN

Sometimes I remember. Most times … I'm confused. … I'm sorry. … I miss those who have left. I sometimes feel … alone.

NATALIE

I think … all of us … at some time … feels alone. (Others nod in agreement) But, I'm right here by you, dad. … Charles.

CHARLES

Of course, you are.

NATALIE

I'm sorry I get impatient. … I love you … Maybe you'd like to find a *new* cat?

CHARLES

With you, daughter, yes. Very much.

BEWILDERED

(After a tearful pause, to CUNNING)

Perhaps two new *executive* positions at Winkles (nodding his attention to Disgruntled and Sarcastic) could also be *'found'* today?

(DISGRUNTLED and SARCASTIC look at CUNNING. Others look at him, too. Moment of silence.)

CUNNING

(Caving) Fine. (Happy reactions) I'll just need their names.

SARCASTIC and DISGRUNTLED
Teri   Terry

(They look at each other in delighted surprise.)

BEWILDERED

(To CUNNING) Thank you, (Mr./Ms.) Winkle. (He hugs his daughter.) I'm proud of you, too, dear.

CUNNING

Call me Peyton. ...And you *should* be proud of...

YOUNG GIRL

...Emily. I'm Emily. And this is my dad. Ben.

PEYTON

You should be proud of Emily, ...Ben. And of yourself. I see that I haven't give you enough credit.

(PEYTON, BEN, EMILY cross to exits for respective movies.)

YOUNG MAN

(To YOUNG LADY) I'm Sam.

YOUNG LADY

I know, silly.

SAM

Well, everyone was introducing themselves, so I thought ... (YOUNG LADY kisses him.)

YOUNG LADY

Colby.

(She wraps her arm around his and pulls him into movie.)

CHARLES

(To WOMAN as he stands*)* On that note ... we, too, have a movie to finish.

NATALIE

(Kindly) Unless you'd prefer to visit the Humane Society.

CHARLES

Oh! I would like that very much. (To EMT, who has begun to leave.) THANK YOU ...

EMT

...Jordan. My pleasure. Take care of each other.

(EMT exits to movie. CHARLES and NATALIE exit SR. TERRY and TERI are now the only people left in the lobby. Pause. Realization.)

TERRY and TERI
What are we wearing these for? What are we standing here for?

(They rip off movie complex vests & run off SR.)

(Lights down.)

One a Day
to the Horizon

Craig Kirchner

April is cruel, and all that,
it's also National Poetry month.
The challenge is one a day,
for thirty days.
It's now May, I write 'April',
next day I write 'Everything',
as you can imagine, I'm tapped.

Sitting, full bellied,
graduated during the challenge,
from pencil to ball point.
I'm also doing yellow legal pad,
something about yellow paper,
makes me feel like I'm lying,
which I am, I'll deal with it.

There's something lounging,
I can feel it just below the surface,
it's like a salamander under a rock,
by the creek, slimy, red spots,
may sun himself, or the water rises,
maybe something moves the rock.
It's a chance it's not a 'he', then what?

There is usually something,
waiting at the horizon,
drive till the car stops running,
or at least until nothing is familiar.
As a child I wanted to fly,
like Icarus, mostly wanted to escape,
the wings didn't melt, I ran out of gas.

Summer Solitude

Karen Colstrom

To the North Pole

John Delaney

The ice was two to three meters thick.
It took us three days in an icebreaker,
leaving from Murmansk, where temperatures
flirted with the sixties. It was freezing,
of course, when we got there, two below
Celsius, to be exact: the middle
of summer with overcast skies
and limited visibility. Not
like the brochure with its beach ball sun.
Still, after all, we made the most of it.

Rangers set off with their rifles
to secure a safe perimeter.
A classic British telephone booth,
lipstick red, popped up in the snow.
I called home on a satellite phone,
but was caught off guard by the machine
that answered. What does one say, except
'guess where I am' and 'sorry I missed you'
when no one's really listening?
And who knew what time it was precisely?

A red carpet led to the dipping hole,
where a few braved the polar chill
in bikinis and cutoffs, posing
for our makeshift paparazzi
as they leaped out on their leashes,
then struggled back to the ladder
with dagger strokes and lockjaw grins.
Reality celebs, they donned thick robes
and tossed back shots of Russian vodka
while loud music bounded across the snow.

Someone with spunk had brought a Santa suit
and cartwheeled and cavorted
over the spiritless white landscape.
We were the hundredth ship to reach true north,
so formed the numerals in linked human chains,
while the moment was captured on video.

Later, I grabbed the ship's anchor line
and tugged dramatically for a snapshot;
others danced around our maypole,
where the world supposedly was spinning.

I thought of the billions below us,
in all directions and predicaments,
working through the day's obstacles.
We stood unclocked above it all,
though I felt guilty and undeserving,
remembering the poor explorers,
their frostbite and scurvy, the hellish
sledging over hummocks and pressure
ridges, facing impossible open leads,
desperate to stake their claim here.

I left my footprints far out from the ship
that looked planted on a blank canvas,
where foreground and background merged.
One day, I thought, they'll be no place to stand.
A bell buoy will mark the spot; then
adventurers will head there to ring it.
So much of life is lived on an east/west
axis, following the rigors of the sun.
But you reach a numb point, much like ours,
where the sun does not set or even run.

The ice pack floats over a deep ocean
and drifts in different directions.
Where we planted our flag will not be north,
exactly, tomorrow: it's a moving
target on the ice, like many
deep-brooded things I can think of—
an explorer's frozen ambition,
a couple's melting glacial love,
the whiteout of forgotten youth.

There was nothing there but that cold hard truth.

A Field of Sunflowers

James P. Cooper

Standing inside a sunflower field,
I seem to have captured their attention
as their heads are turned toward me.

Too little space to dance for them,
I begin telling jokes. Their stalks move
in the wind as if they clap at each joke.

Laughing too hard, they let their pollen
fall like tears onto their leaves. Undisturbed,
bees fly from one head to another.

When I step out of the field, the sunflowers
still look in the same direction
as if expecting another performance.

It will be hours before they cover their heads,
before cumulus clouds drift over the field.
I promise to return the next day

with a bagful of jokes. I walk away but glance
back to find their heads seem a little brighter,
their stalks a little straighter, their leaves waving.

Inside a Field of Sunflowers

James P. Cooper

Missing Half

Cecil Sayre

Maybe I did not hug my father enough
after his wife, my mother, died.
What we were doing all those hours
sitting in his apartment, talking about nothing,
waiting for those moments of silence to pass?
Why did we not rest our heads on each other's shoulders,
bury our faces in each other's neck,
and cry?

Today I can no longer count the number of pills
I found in and under his chair,
a number I thought I would always remember,
kneeling on the floor in front of him,
the pills in my hand,
asking questions no man could answer
but with a shrug, a weak gesture,
a showing of empty hands.

The weeks before his death
his fingers fluttered and fumbled with the air above him,
too weak to open an aspirin bottle.
I would hold his hands in mine to still them,
but his body did not know stillness again
until he was laid in his casket,
a body smaller than the man I remember
towering over me. Yet still.
Maybe I did not hug him enough.

The Riot Makers

Pawel Grajnert

A screenplay based on "The Pardoner's Tale" by Geoffrey Chaucer

EXT. WISCONSIN FARMHOUSE DAY
A sunny morning in farm country.

A motorcycle is parked next to a tree behind the farm house. A window opens.
PETER, 20s, with his clothes barely on, jumps out the window while he pulls on a leather jacket.

A YOUNG WOMAN, 20s, naked, looks out after him. She's pulled inside.

A FARMER, 50s, aims a shot gun at PETER. PETER runs. The FARMER shoots. The ground around PETER is peppered with shot. The FARMER reloads.

PETER jumps on his bike, starts it and rides away. The FARMER aims, but PETER is already out of range.

EXT. WISCONSIN COUNTRY ROAD DAY

PETER on his bike. He rides down a paved highway through a rolling hilly landscape on a bright Midwestern big-sky day.

Two bikes roar over a hill behind PETER.

BILL, 40s, slim and bald, and SAM, 40s, chubby and long- haired, each with a leather jacket on, pull either side of PETER.

On the back of all three jackets: The Riot Makers. The trio ride toward a small Wisconsin town.

EXT. MAIN STREET - SMALL WISCONSIN TOWN DAY
The trio ride down a deserted street and pass a hardware store.

INT. TAVERN DAY
The trio enter the empty tavern. A BARTENDER stands behind the counter.

> BILL
> Well, let's get some drinks into us and see if you got any leaks.

> SAM
> Bartender. Bourbon. Three.

The BARTENDER pours the drinks. The three bikers raise their glasses and gulp the whisky.

SAM (CONT'D)

So you had a good time.

PETER

Oh, yeah.

SAM

And that's all you got.

BILL

The farmer's daughter.

PETER

Yeah.

BILL

So you got nothing to share with us.

SAM

Except a story.

PETER

Hey... I...

SAM

You know, Bill and I have enough stories of our own.

PETER

I'm sorry guys.

BILL

"I'm sorry guys."

SAM

That ain't gonna keep our outfit outfitted.

BILL

You understand.

SAM

He understands.

PETER

Yeah.

BILL

We like to see cash in the morning.

SAM

Every morning.

PETER

Every morning.

                              BILL
    Bartender, another round.

                              SAM
    On our young friend here.

The BARTENDER pours three more drinks. PETER pays.

                         SAM (CONT'D)
    Where the hell is everyone.

                           BARTENDER
    Not here.

                              BILL
    Now tip the man well.

PETER leaves some more cash on the counter.

                           BARTENDER
    They're at the funeral.

                              BILL
    Funeral.

                           BARTENDER
    You know the guy.

                              SAM
    I do.

                           BARTENDER
    Larry Benson.

                              BILL
    Larry Benson. He was a young man.

                           BARTENDER
    About your age.

                              SAM
    How'd he die.

                           BARTENDER
    They found him just out back a couple days ago. Stabbed. Bled white.

                             PETER
    Stabbed.

                           BARTENDER
    Guy who did it left that burnt rubber skid mark out front.

                              BILL
You seen him.

                            BARTENDER
Just his back.

                              SAM
Did you recognize him.

                            BARTENDER
Lone wolf.

                              BILL
What'd he ride.

                            BARTENDER
Rat bike, never heard an engine like he had before either. And I heard them all.

                              BILL
Anything.

BILL takes money from PETER's pile and pushes it across the bar.

                            BARTENDER
Looked like he had ape hangers. They say he's the same one that did in that family over on Stillwater Lane off of County D. Got everyone: Husband, wife, two young kids, even the grandma.

                              PETER
Hell.

                            BARTENDER
They say he calls himself Death.

                              SAM
Death.

                            BARTENDER
Bastard stopped just outside of town and waved. Then he just rode on. Went West.

                              BILL
Pour us three more.

BILL pushes some money toward the BARTENDEr who pours out the drinks.

BILL raises his glass.

                          BILL (CONT'D)
To the Riot Makers. Death is dead.

SAM and PETER raise their glasses.

                    SAM   PETER (at the same time)
Death is dead.

EXT. TAVERN DAY
The three bikers peel away and leave a cloud of blue smoke behind.

EXT. WISCONSIN HIGHWAY DAY
The three bikers zoom down the road and past a 'County D' sign.

EXT. COUNTY D DAY
The three bikers take a fast turn off of County D onto Stillwater Lane, a gravel road.

EXT. STILLWATER LANE DAY
The bikers pass a farm that's for sale.

EXT. STILLWATER LANE - BRIDGE DAY
A horse-drawn Amish wagon crosses the narrow bridge.

The bikes slowly come around a turn and approach.

EXT. STILLWATER LANE - ON BRIDGE DAY

The bikers pull up in front of the wagon and block its way. Bill revs his engine.

                           SAM
     Hey you.

The wagon stops.

An OLD MAN, 80s, bent down and emaciated, with white hair and beard; an Amish farmer in a wide brimmed hat and dark cotton clothes looks up, smiles, points to his ears and shakes his head.

BILL turns his bike's motor off. PETER and SAM follow suit.

                        OLD MAN
     Peace be with you, young gentleman.

                          BILL
     What are you doing out here all alone old man.

                        OLD MAN
     It seems that death has not taken me. So I travel on.

                         PETER
     Travel.

                        OLD MAN
     Though I go from town to town, farm to farm across this continent far and wide, I have yet
     to find a single person who would exchange his youth to have the wisdom of my age.

                         PETER
     Get out of our way crazy old man.

OLD MAN

If you should be so lucky as to live as long as me, would you then want someone to speak to you in the manner in which you now speak to me.

PETER

Just move.

SAM

You said you've seen Death around here.

BILL

You better tell us where Death is old man.

OLD MAN

By a lone oak in a wide field just left at the next turn off this very road. Death will not be hard to find for the likes of you.

PETER

You better believe it.

SAM starts his bike.

The OLD MAN gets his wagon out of the bikers' way and watches them cross to the other side of the bridge.

PETER looks back in his rear-view mirror.

The OLD MAN waves as his wagon disappears behind a cloud of dust.

EXT. A FIELD DAY
A lone tree stands in a wide field. The bikers ride up, stop and dismount.

EXT. TREE IN FIELD DAY
The three bikers approach the tree.

There's nothing there but a ladder that leads up to a hunting blind in the tree's lower branches.

BILL

Hey, Death.

SAM

See what's up there.

PETER climbs the ladder.

PETER (O.S.)

Oh my God.

SAM

What.

BILL

Is he up there?

PETER

You got to see it to believe it.

EXT. ON BLIND DAY
SAM, BILL and PETER stand and look at a pile of gold bars.

PETER

Who the hell would leave a pile of gold out here.

BILL

Who the hell cares.

SAM

We're gonna need a cage.

SAM (CONT'D)

Go get one from town.

PETER

Me.

BILL	SAM
Yeah, you.	We can't move this on our bikes.

EXT. TAVERN AFTERNOON
PETER pulls up in front of the tavern.

INT. TAVERN AFTERNOON
PETER enters.

BARTENDER

Did you find the bastard.

PETER

Still lookin' for him. Get me a bottle of whiskey.

PETER places a couple hundred dollar bills on the counter.

BARTENDER

You got it. Those geezers still treatin' you like dirt.

PETER

Been treated worse.

PETER places another hundred dollar bill on the counter.

PETER (CONT'D)

I've never been here.

BARTENDER

I understand.

The BARTENDER puts the bottle of whiskey on the bar. PETER pushes the keys to his bike across the counter.

                              PETER
        And that bike should disappear.

The BARTENDER takes the keys.

                           BARTENDER
        What bike.

PETER grabs the whiskey and heads toward the back of the tavern.

EXT. BACK OF TAVERN AFTERNOON
PETER steps out of the tavern and stops.

In front of him - a dried puddle of blood covered with feasting flies. He steps around the blood and leaves.

EXT. SMALL TOWN STREET AFTERNOON
PETER passes the hardware store. It's closed.

EXT. SMALL TOWN ALLEY AFTERNOON
PETER smashes a window and climbs through it.

INT. HARDWARE STORE AFTERNOON
PETER picks up a hammer. A screw driver. He quickly walks toward the back of the store when he stops and looks: A box with a skull on it and the word POISON in bold letters above that.

PETER examines the box.

FLASH FORWARD
EXT. TREE DAY
SAM and BILL sit against the tree. SAM takes a long gulp from the whiskey bottle. He passes it on to BILL who takes a long drink.

PETER climbs down from the blind with a couple gold bars in his hands and places them in the trunk of a car.

                              BILL
        You want a drink.

                              PETER
        I'll drink when I'm done.

                              BILL
        This boy knows what's what.

                              SAM
        And who's who.

SAM takes the bottle from BILL and drinks.

END FLASH FORWARD

INT/EXT. CAR ON COUNTY D EVE
PETER drives down the road in a car. The screwdriver sticks out of the ignition.

He drinks from the bottle of whiskey. He places it between his legs. He tears open the box of poison and pours the powder inside into the bottle.

EXT. COUNTY D EVE
The car takes the turn onto Stillwater Lane.

I/E. CAR ON STILLWATER LANE EVE
PETER drives on.

FLASH FORWARD
EXT. TREE DAY
PETER carries a gold bar and places it into the trunk full of gold. PETER looks at all the gold and smiles. He looks behind himself.

SAM and BILL lie against the tree, eyes closed, the empty bottle of whiskey next to Bill.

SAM and BILL are totally still.

PETER approaches and kicks SAM. He doesn't budge.

END FLASH FORWARD

I/E. CAR ON STILLWATER LANE - AT FARM THAT'S FOR SALE EVE
PETER smiles.

EXT. STILLWATER LANE EVE
The car passes the farm that's for sale.

EXT. TREE IN FIELD EVE
Insect buzz fills the quiet of a still early evening, SAM and BILL lie against the tree. Eyes closed.

Car noise breaks the quiet. SAM opens his eyes. He wakes BILL.

EXT. FIELD EVE
The car drives onto the field.

EXT. UNDER TREE IN FIELD EVE
The car stops.

SAM and BILL are on their feet and approach.

                              SAM
         It's good to see you.

PETER gets out of the car.

PETER

You, too.

He tosses the bottle of whiskey to SAM. It's three quarters full.

BILL

Started without us.

PETER

Couldn't help myself.

BILL takes a swig and hands it to SAM, who drinks.

PETER (CONT'D)

Let's get that gold and the hell out of here.

PETER climbs the ladder, Bill hands PETER the bottle.

EXT. ON BLIND EVENING
PETER takes the bottle up from BILL, hides out of view on the blind and doesn't drink.

After a moment PETER hands the bottle back to BILL.

PETER

I'll throw down the bars.

BILL takes a drink and hands the bottle to SAM. PETER tosses down the first bar.

EXT. UNDER TREE IN FIELD NIGHT
BILL puts a bar in the trunk of the car.

SAM comes up behind him and hands him the bottle one quarter full.

BILL drinks.

PETER joins them and places a bar in the trunk full of gold.

PETER

That's it, that's the last one.

BILL

You want a drink.

PETER

Yeah.

PETER slowly lifts the bottle towards his lips but stops. SAM has stuck him with a knife in the back. SAM pulls it out. Blood stains PETER's shirt.

SAM

Sorry kid, half the gold is more than a third.

Then BILL stabs PETER in his belly and takes the bottle from PETER's hand as PETER collapses.

BILL
>   Wouldn't want to waste any of that.

BILL drinks and hands the bottle to SAM who also drinks.

EXT. UNDER TREE IN FIELD MORNING
PETER's body lies in the grass next to the car.

Next to his body are BILL's and SAM's the empty bottle of whiskey next to SAM's hand.

Flies buzz around their bodies.

A LITTLE GIRL, 7, in a sun dress, straddles a bicycle and looks at them.

She turns and rides away onto the field.

EXT. FIELD DAY
She stops. Turns. Smiles. And waves to the camera.

I Am My Mother's Shadow

Karyn M. Bruce

I buried her in a poem thirteen years after she died.
The five days of mourning neatly fitting into stanzas
of the emptiness that filled me. The words carefully chosen,
like those of the priest who never knew her, but thought
she was a godly woman, speaking about her as if her soul
had visited him in his sleep, a speech better coming from
the bartenders and cronies who slopped their words
in cheap whiskey, everything black and twisted, like the silence
that followed me in and out of nightmares. She was there,
after I wrote the poem, waking me from sleep, the chill of the room
wrapping me in fear. And I saw her, dressed in the hollowness
of what death can do, watching me, perhaps, in sadness of the words
that defined her, there in the shadows of who I had become. Without her.

Vanishing Hare

Karen Colstrom

What My Mom Doesn't Say

Elly Katz

She wears paragraphs on her face,
streams of soundless sentences steady there in
reeds of muscles at cheek bones,
hiking the capsized hill of a chin,
skewing the balance of lenses across
the bridge of the nose.

It's all there— screwed tight in
measured
buckets of loss.

Menisci rupture,
surface-tension crying
with overflow.

Prayers go unaddressed,
marked with missing postage or
accidentally mailed to the wrong God.

Her face is sentinel to my face,
to what I cannot face,
what I must efface, if only for a
heartbeat.

Here, wear this for me—
a trillion tons of grief sinking me,
I didn't have to beg
across the silence.

Yes, that's how I will breathe,
even if I seethe.

I will carry that too,
she didn't have to say, because her
speechlessness said it
before the longing crossed
grooves inside me.

Eastern Europe #12g

Kenneth Kesner

Late Love

Sharon Scholl

After sixty years love turns to sympathy,
a symmetry of suffering
one breaking body to another.

Lust shrinks to every night's embrace,
a clasp of hands, a shoulder hug,
whispered wish for restful sleep.

No need for entertainment,
just books, a nap, summer afternoons
watching squirrels scamper up the trees.

Days assume the rhythm of a heartbeat,
a comforting facsimile of life
tinged by the shadow of its ending.

Death's dread is nothing mythical
but knowing our twinned lives will cease,
leaving only half a being.

Mrs. Nash

Ruth J. Heflin

A Dramatization of the first historically documented
EuroAmerican male to live his life as a woman
in the style of Alfred Hitchcock

FADE IN:
INT FORT RILEY OFFICERS BALLROOM EVENING
The year is 1878. A military band plays, and a young tenor sings, "I'll Take You Home Again, Kathleen" by Thomas P. Westendorf, as Cavalry officers mingle and dance with colorfully dressed women. MARIA STRAW and CAPT. BENJAMIN STRAW are in attendance. Flags and displays of arms festoon the room, which isn't crowded since only a sprinkling of people have shown up. One woman in her mid-thirties, MRS. NASH, because she is tall, angular, yet attractive, stands out. She finishes a dance with a young officer, and, at her request, they move over to the refreshment table. She motions to a chair, moving to sit in it rather quickly. People notice. She smiles and waves off attention, gratefully accepting the punch her young officer hands her. She sips the punch, pulls out her fan and tries to appear well, but her hands tremble. Making excuses, she leaves the room.

EXT VERANDA OUTSIDE BALLROOM EVENING
MRS. NASH makes her way slowly down the veranda outside the ballroom, past one or two people, to the stairs. She stops, steadies herself, and leans heavily on the rail as she descends the stairs.

INT THE BALLROOM EVENING
The dancing continues.

EXT FORT RILEY PARADE GROUNDS EVENING
MRS. NASH crosses the grounds, still alone, slowly.

INT THE BALLROOM EVENING
The dancing continues.

EXT WASHINGTON AVENUE, FORT RILEY EVENING
We see the street and yard in front of a large stone townhouse. Gas lamps are lit along the street. MRS. NASH makes her way across the yard and up the steps, pausing only briefly on the stairs--obviously in physical discomfort.

INT THE BALLROOM SAME EVENING
The dancing continues. A younger, heavy set woman, MARIA STRAW, moves over and whispers to her husband, CAPT. BENJAMIN STRAW, who is standing with other officers. He distractedly waves her on her way. She hurriedly, yet taking the time to smile politely at people she passes, leaves through the same door MRS. NASH did.

INT BEDROOM SAME EVENING
MRS. NASH pours water from a pitcher and tries to cool her head and wrists. Sitting on the
edge of the bed, she bends over to pull off her button-up shoes. Dizzy, she straightens up trying
to regain her balance, instead falls forward onto the floor.

EXT PORCH ROOF OF TOWNHOUSE SAME EVENING
We see through the second story window, having a view of the top half of the staircase, all of the
hallway, and part of the bedroom interior. MARIA mounts the stairs and turns down the
hallway. She enters the bedroom, finds MRS. NASH prostrate, while we see only part of MRS.
NASH's body; the rest is obscured by the view of the bed. MARIA bends down to check her.
The singing and music, which have been heard all this time, stop.

                              MARIA
                            (groaning)
        Oh, no.

INT FORT RILEY UNDERTAKER'S WORKROOM MORNING
The room is brightly lit by windows on two sides. The floors are wooden and heavily worn. The
walls are white washed, but there is no air of sterility or particular cleanliness to the room. The
military UNDERTAKER, a young staff sergeant who looks very boyish, almost effeminate, is
finishing his breakfast and humming the hymn, "Hiding in Thee" by Ira David Sankey and
William O. Cushing, as he enters the room. He sets the remainder of his egg sandwich on the
sheet covering the corpse of MRS. NASH, which is on the table in the center of the room, as he
pulls the sheet partly down to reveal the face. His hand scrapes against what feels like stubble.
He looks closer at the corpse's face and is briefly puzzled by what appears to be beard growth.
He checks the slip of paper under MRS. NASH's head, then seems to almost smile as he runs a
finger down the jaw line. Holding the egg sandwich in his mouth, he pulls the sheet the rest of
the way off. As he finishes the sandwich, he removes her shoes, already partly undone, then
moves to the top of the table to begin unbuttoning her dress. He notices a similar stubble on
the chest, and a notable absence of breasts, just stuffing inside the corset. Presently, he
removes the underwear and his suspicions are confirmed.

                            UNDERTAKER
                        (with a quiet laugh)
        So, Mrs. Nash you are a man.

INT A DARKENED BEDROOM IN BOSTON, MASS.--1873 NIGHT
The sounds of lovers accompany the movement of sheets, which is slightly obscured by the
large bedposts and drapes of a canopy bed. The bedroom door opens suddenly and light stabs
across the bed.

                        ABRAHAM WRIGHT (OS)
        Claypool? Clay, is that you?

A man, ABRAHAM WRIGHT, in his 50s enters the room with a candelabra in one hand and a
pistol in the other. He approaches the bed, where the sounds and movements have stopped.

                        ABRAHAM (CONT)
        I know you're there, Claypool Wright. Show yourself like a man.

A young, bearded man in his early 20s, CLAYPOOL WRIGHT, gets out of the bed and stands
beside the backside of the bed, covering himself with a sheet. The bed's other occupant remains
completely covered.

ABRAHAM (CONT)
I knew it, you...you...bastard. (pause) No, I can't call you that; it'd dishonor the woman who bore you.

ABRAHAM begins to circle the bed, trying to direct the light from the candelabra to get a view of the young man and the bed's other occupant, who remains hidden in the dark. CLAYPOOL/CLAY approaches him, holding out a hand as if to stop him.

CLAYPOOL WRIGHT
Father, don't. You don't understand.

ABRAHAM
Don't call me that. You're no son of mine.

CLAY
Don't....It's not like you think. It's...

ABRAHAM
You...you...sodomite. You'll pay for your sins. Both of you will pay.

ABRAHAM turns the pistol toward the figure sitting under the sheets and fires. The figure under the sheet drops to the bed. CLAY lunges for the gun, struggling to wrestle it out of his father's hand. The candelabra drops to the floor. ABRAHAM screams as though burned, releasing the gun in his effort to get away from his son's touch. He continually wipes his hands over his arms and hands where CLAY touched him.

ABRAHAM (CONT)
Don't ever come near me again. Don't ever look at me again. As far as I'm concerned, you're dead.

ABRAHAM runs from the room. CLAY turns toward the bed, picking up the candelabra to see better. A man in his 40s, PROFESSOR EDWARD NEISMAN, shivers there, unharmed by the bullet. He reaches for CLAY. They embrace.

EXT   HARVARD GROUNDS   DAY
Snow covers the ground. Sidewalks are shoveled clean. CLAY, a long dark coat wrapped about him, waits on a bench. NEISMAN, wearing a black don's robe and carrying a large black valise, exits a building and heads in CLAY's direction. They walk across the grounds together. Their breath steams as they talk.

CLAY
(gravely)

Leaving?

NEISMAN
Voluntarily removing myself from the esteemed, and enlightened, Harvard grounds.
(looks around)
Not that I want to teach here now. I won't teach anywhere in New England again.

CLAY
What will you do? You can't go south.

                              NEISMAN
No, I'll probably head west. California maybe. And you?

                                CLAY
Father's cut off my income, but Mother sent me enough to last awhile. I can't...go
anywhere else.

                              NEISMAN
How will you support yourself?

                                CLAY
My best friend, Charles Stallard, has agreed to let me stay with him for a while. His
parents have always been fond of me. I can probably manage for awhile.

                              NEISMAN
And if they find out?

                                CLAY
Try to convince them it's not true.

                              NEISMAN
                               (stops)
Can you convince yourself? You know you can't live without...X, as Tchaikovsky calls it.
You haven't chosen it; it's chosen you. You'll want such a relationship, as we had, again.
You know you will.

                                CLAY
                          (uncomfortable)
I'm not like you. I don't need... anything. I'll get along just fine.

NEISMAN looks at him skeptically and steps into a waiting carriage. CLAY watches the
carriage leave before crossing the street.

EXT BOSTON OPERA HOUSE NIGHT
Snow falls. Carriages pull up and release extravagantly dressed occupants. CLAY, with a young
woman on his arm (TILLY OSGOOD), disembarks behind another couple (CHARLES
STALLARD and date). They enter.

INT ENTRANCE HALL OF OPERA HOUSE
CLAY checks his hat and coat at the cloak room, flirting with the coat check girl. Takes TILLY's
arm again. An older man, recognizing CLAY, stops, watches CLAY, whispers to his wife, and
hustles her inside while she tries to look at CLAY. CHARLES notices the attention.

                             CHARLES
                          (nudging Clay)
Did you see that? Old Professor Hill seemed to sniff something peculiar.
                          (indicating TILLY)
You haven't tainted this young woman's reputation already, have you?

                                CLAY
                              (smiles)
No, not yet.

                                    TILLY
                                  (giggles)
Oh, stop it, you two. Professor Hill was probably just noticing my new fur. He's
probably the old stuffy type who doesn't think young women should dress so flashily.

                                   CHARLES
                        (smiling and winking at CLAY)
Yes, I'm sure you're right. How could anyone think Mr. Claypool Wright had anything but
honorable intentions toward any woman?

EXT OUTSIDE A BOSTON BALLROOM   NIGHT
Carriages pull up and release extravagantly dressed occupants.

INT ENTRYWAY TO A BOSTON BALLROOM   NIGHT
CLAY, TILLY, CHARLES and a new date enter boisterously, shaking snow off their coats. All
check their apparel with an attendant and enter the main ballroom.

INT MAIN BALLROOM SAME NIGHT
CLAY and TILLY begin to dance immediately to a Tchaikovsky waltz. CHARLES and his date
separate--she heads toward a group of women, he to a group of men.

CHARLES' date enters the group of six women, all in their late teens, early twenties,
exuberantly.

                          FIRST WOMAN IN GROUP
          Don't tell us you came here with them.

                               CHARLES' DATE
          With whom?

                               SECOND WOMAN
          With Claypool Wright and his lot.

                               CHARLES' DATE
                                  (puzzled)
          Yes, of course.

                                FIRST WOMAN
          Poor thing. Haven't you heard?

CHARLES nonchalantly lights a cigar before approaching his cronies, six men about his own
age.

                                 FIRST MAN
          How is everything, Stallard?

                                  CHARLES
          Fine, Wallace. And you?

                                SECOND MAN
          Still faithful to Wright, I see.

                                  CHARLES
          Faithful?

FIRST MAN
Oh, come now, Stallard. Surely, you've heard the rumors.

CHARLES
Since when do you listen to gossip, Wallace?

THIRD MAN
Claypool Wright is a fine young man, I'm sure. But you know how rumors thrive in
Boston. Wagging tails keep tales wagging, if you know what I mean.

CLAY and TILLY finish a waltz and move toward the refreshment room. People watch them,
moving out of their way politely.

INT REFRESHMENT ROOM   SAME NIGHT

TILLY
(giggles)
They think we're a scandal, don't they?

CLAY
Does that bother you?

TILLY
No, except that...

CLAY
Except that, what?

TILLY
Father says I shouldn't see you anymore. He says he doesn't like the way people are
beginning to talk about you.

CLAY
(feigning innocence)
About me?

TILLY
I suppose you've tarnished too many women's reputations.

CLAY
You don't seem to mind.

TILLY
I've never been noticed this much before. I always feel as though I'm somebody with
you.

CLAY
(looking around)
As you are, Tilly.
(in a fierce whisper)
And what would you do if I kissed you right now?

TILLY

I'd...blush. But I'd probably love it.

CLAY sweeps TILLY into an elaborate embrace and kiss. Many people watch, some with elaborate disgust, others with obvious relief and amusement. CHARLES watches from just inside the doorway.

INT DINING ROOM OF STALLARD MANSION EVENING
Large, dark, heavy drapes completely cover large windows along one side of the room. A fairly long table, ornately set and surrounded by highbacked Victorian furniture, and a long sideboard along the wall opposite the windows, completely covered by silver trays laden with food, take up a good deal of the room. A large marble fireplace fills the end opposite the double doorway. A BUTLER slides the doors open and several well-dressed people enter and find their specified seats around the table. CLAY has TILLY and another young woman at each arm. CHARLES is escorting his mother and another older woman. MR. STALLARD is talking with his colleague, the older woman's husband.

MR. STALLARD

Louisiana's sugar crop this year was less than a third what it was twenty years ago. Charles says what with all the negroes moving north and west to find employment there's no one to work the fields anymore.

COLLEAGUE

If Hawaii hadn't increased its production, prices would be soaring now.

MRS. STALLARD

Yes, but do we want to eat sugar made at a place filled with so many lepers?

CHARLES

Now, mother. I've told you the lepers are separate from the cane growers.

CLAY

What we really have to worry about are these Populists.

MR. STALLARD

Poor Southerners who've moved West for free land. Free land. You'd think the government had more sense. Some of them have got so much land now they think they're rich men.

TILLY

I thought having land meant they were rich.

Everyone pauses to look at TILLY. The older men smile at her politely. CHARLES looks at her as though she's meddled again, then looks at CLAY, who smiles and shrugs. MRS. STALLARD looks around the table, wiping her mouth with her napkin, then motions for the BUTLER to bring more food from the sideboard.

COLLEAGUE
(under his breath)
Having land didn't help the Indians.

INT DRAWING ROOM OF THE STALLARD MANSION NIGHT
The men, CHARLES, his father, CLAY, and another man, have been smoking after dinner. CHARLES' father engages the fourth man in moderate conversation as they are seated in

comfortable chairs near the fireplace. CHARLES and CLAY have been standing, leaning against the backs of tall chairs, at a respectable distance, listening to the two older men converse. CLAY exhales cigar smoke and nods toward the two older men.

CLAY

That's how we'll be some day.

CHARLES
(as out of a reverie)

Excuse me?

CLAY

Like them. Two old men contemplating the demise of the world over good cigars as our dinners digest.

CHARLES

Yes, possibly.
(looks Clay over seriously)
You think we'll be...friends, I mean, as good of friends as we are now...always?

CLAY
(shifting closer, affectionately)

Don't you?

CHARLES
(motioning Clay further from the fire)
Not that I mind, you understand, but father's been worrying at me about it. I mean it doesn't look good for him to take in a young man of questionable reputation, you know. Especially with your father being a respectable lawyer, a partner of Leeds, Carey, and Wright, after all. Mr. Wright's judgment isn't likely to be questioned and father's concerned how he, how he and I...

CLAY
(curtly)

What is it, Charles?

CHARLES

Is there any chance of your father's taking you back?

CLAY
(stiffening)
No. None. I've told you that before. Look, as soon as I get taken on by a firm, I'll leave. I know I've been a financial burden to you and your father, but...

CHARLES

It's not that.

CLAY

What then?

CHARLES

Don't you know?

                              CLAY
Don't I know what?

                            CHARLES
People have been talking.

                              CLAY
Yes, well, I know people are unkind about my financial situation, but...

                            CHARLES
No, it's more than that.

                              CLAY
What then?

                            CHARLES
There's talk that you were expelled from Harvard for...well, for
some...unsavory...actions.

                              CLAY
Unsavory?

CHARLES steps closer. Their voices take on a more intimate tone as they occasionally glance
toward the older men.

                            CHARLES
Were you involved with Professor Neisman?

                              CLAY
Involved?

                            CHARLES
                      (almost conspiratorily)
Were you?

CLAY smiles and takes a long drag from his cigar.

MONTAGE:
EXT OUTSIDE BOSTON OPERA HOUSE NIGHT
CHARLES and a new date disembark a cab. Snow on ground shows signs of beginning to melt
away.

INT JUST INSIDE OPERA ENTRANCE SAME NIGHT
CLAY is checking his hat and coat, as TILLY stands by. TILLY smiles happily at CHARLES, as
he and his date enter, and waves. CHARLES maneuvers his date over to the other side of the
entrance. CLAY escorts a puzzled TILLY inside.

INT MAIN BALLROOM NIGHT
CLAY and TILLY enter. Everyone seems to stop and stare. TILLY beams; CLAY is
uncomfortable. They head to the refreshment room and people part noticeably to get out of
their way.

EXT OUTSIDE THE OSGOOD BROWNSTONE NIGHT

CLAY rings the bell. A MAID answers. Shakes her head. He becomes insistent. She starts to close the door on him. He tries to stop her. A BUTLER intervenes, imposingly. CLAY, disgusted, leaves. TILLY watches from an upper window.

EXT OUTSIDE THE BOSTON OPERA HOUSE NIGHT
It's raining heavily, but the flow of patrons is as heavy as ever. CLAY disembarks a cab, but he is stopped by a DOOR ATTENDANT. After a brief discussion, the ATTENDANT steps away to help someone else exit a cab. Dumbfounded because he's been told not to enter, CLAY stands out in the rain. Eventually moving away because people begin to stare.

EXT OUTSIDE THE BOSTON BALLROOM NIGHT
The pre-spring wind is heavy, causing skirts to flap like flags. CLAY disembarks a cab and is greeted by coldness from other patrons, none of whom return his greetings.

INT ENTRYWAY TO BALLROOM SAME NIGHT
Even the COAT CHECK GIRL is cool toward him. People make an obvious effort not to be near him.

INT MAIN BALLROOM SAME NIGHT
CLAY approaches a group of young men, who make an obvious effort to shun him. Across the room, TILLY, who is with CHARLES, muffles tears in a handkerchief as she's escorted into another room. She looks longingly after CLAY. An ATTENDANT approaches CLAY with his coat. The ATTENDANT starts an explanation, but CLAY waves him off in disgust. With one last look around, CLAY takes his coat, tosses it over one arm, and steps out into the wind.

EXT THE RED LIGHT DISTRICT OF BOSTON NIGHT
CLAY, slightly tipsy, walks down the street looking closely at all the women. One woman, VERA, nearly as tall as CLAY and large boned (she should have strongly masculine features), attracts his attention the most. CLAY follows her actions from across the street, not certain she's a prostitute. She smiles at a man passing by. He ignores her. She fluffs up her the flounced material on her dress' bustle, and notices CLAY watching her. Placing her hands firmly on her hips, she begins to swing them as she walks down the street. Finally, he approaches her.

                    CLAY
Excuse me, madam. Are you a lady of the evening?

                 PROSTITUTE
              (doesn't lose a beat)
It's evening, isn't it? And I'm obviously a lady. Right?

                    CLAY
               (looks her over)
Well...

                 PROSTITUTE
         (straightening to her full height)
What do you mean, well?

                    CLAY
               (backs up a bit)
Of course, madam. I only meant to say that...that...you're a very striking woman.

                        PROSTITUTE
                      (softens a bit)
Why...thank you...sir.
                 (runs a hand through his hair)
You're a very striking man, if it's not too forward for me to say so.

                          CLAY
No. Not at all. Listen. I'm really rather new at all of this, you see. I'm not sure...

                        PROSTITUTE
                   (puts finger to his lips)
Then you need little Vera's guided tour, dear.

VERA leads him away to her bordello still concentrating on swinging her hips as though they're
tied to a lease pulling him along.

EXT   BORDELLO   SAME NIGHT
Several women stand or sit on the steps. Many men and women enter and leave the building, a
large brick house that appears to have been an early version of a mansion. VERA leads CLAY
up the steps and through the front door.

INT   BORDELLO ENTRANCE HALL   SAME NIGHT
VERA waves to her MADAM, who seems somewhat surprised VERA has a guest. The MADAM,
a tiny woman with very thin features, shouts out a room number above the din of music and
laughter. CLAY tries to watch all the commotion in the adjacent rooms, but VERA hurriedly
leads him upstairs still keeping up the hip-swing.

INT   BORDELLO BEDROOM   SAME NIGHT
The room is decorated in frills and bright colors. A Virgin Mary statuette sits on the mantle. A
crucifix hangs on the wall above the bed. VERA leads CLAY to the bed and begins undressing
him and herself. He tries stopping her several times, but she doesn't understand and persists.
Finally, when she's down to basics, but he's still mostly dressed, he sits abruptly on the bed and
covers his face. Puzzled, she sits next to him and pulls his hands away from his face.

                          VERA
                        (shocked)
Why, you're crying. It's okay, honey, there's no need to cry about it.

                          CLAY
You don't understand.

                          VERA
Why, sure I do. I'm touched by it, really. I've never had a man cry when I've undressed
in front of him before.
                    (cups his chin in her palm)
Is this your first time?

CLAY begins laughing. He pats VERA's leg, then realizes it's bare and gets up to drape the
coverlet of the bed around VERA's body.

                          CLAY
You don't understand, Vera. I'm...I'm not...that kind of man.

VERA

How many kinds of men are there?

CLAY

I thought I could. I really thought I could. But I can't.

VERA
(income vanishing)

Ain't I pretty enough?

CLAY hugs her, laughing. She's startled, looks around puzzled, and finally hugs him back, catching his laughter.

CLAY

You're gorgeous, Vera.

VERA
(pulling back)

I'm not the brightest woman in the world, but I don't get it.

CLAY laughs heartily, pulls her toward him again, giving her a bear hug. She feels something sticking her in his jacket pocket and reaches in to pull out two cigars. CLAY takes one, bites off the tip, motions for VERA to do the same, and they light up off of his lighter, laughing giddily as VERA chokes on the smoke.

INT   A CHEAP HOTEL ROOM   MORNING
Clay wakes looking haggard, but cheerful. He gets up from his double-sized bed and crosses to the mirror hung above the washstand. The only other pieces of furniture in the room are a large wardrobe with a long bottom drawer and a chair. As he rubs his hand over his stubble and looks at himself almost in disbelief, he hears a commotion outside. He crosses to the window, which he opens and leans out.

EXT   STREET BELOW HOTEL WINDOW   MORNING
This is a working district, and several delivery wagons have collided causing a traffic jam. While men yell at each other in the street over the incident, women move quickly along the sidewalks, many carrying baskets of clothing.

CLAY is surprised to see VERA, the prostitute, carrying such a basket as she crosses the street toward his hotel.

CLAY
(leaning out window)

Vera! Vera! Up here. Wait. What are you doing?

VERA
(glancing up)

Mr. Wright. Is that you? Be careful, you're going to fall!

CLAY
(sits on sill)

Why don't you come up to talk to me?

I've got work to do, dear. Mrs. Vandercleven expects her wash back this morning and I've got to pick up her dirties, as well as get Mrs. McDevon's clear over in...

CLAY

Laundry? When did you start doing laundry? I thought you...

VERA
(waves her hands)
Dear Mr. Wright...
(looks around)
A woman's got to make a decent living, you know. Enough gabbing, dear, I've got to be going. Mrs. Vandercleven won't wait all morning.

CLAY

Wait. I'll come with you.

VERA

What ever for?

CLAY
(smiles)
I like your company.

VERA
(smiles)
Very well then. Come along, if you're coming.

EXT   A MORE POSH STREET IN BOSTON   MORNING
CLAY is now carrying the basket of clothing. VERA seems uncomfortable with this fact, worried she'll be seen by her employer. She directs CLAY onto a back street.

EXT   THE ALLEYWAY   SAME MORNING
CLAY sees the high fences and brick walls for the first time, never having spent much time in areas frequented by servants. They pass other delivery people, making way for the milkwagon. VERA nods and responds to greetings by others. She nods toward a large young woman in a tight black dress and small white apron shaking rugs at the back of one residence.

VERA
See her? The vixen. She used to work the streets like I do and now she's an upstairs maid, of all things.
(whispers conspiratorially)
I hear she gives it free to the master of the house.
(pauses dramatically)
And his son.

CLAY

It lets her keep her job, doesn't it?

VERA

The boy's only thirteen!

                              CLAY
                            (smiles)
I did it with the upstairs maid once.

                              VERA
                           (surprised)
You?

                              CLAY
                            (nods)
Hated it. She had these huge breasts...
                         (makes hand gesture of size)
and I nearly suffocated in them.

                              VERA
                            (laughs)
Dear, you didn't have to put your face there, you know.

                              CLAY
                            (laughs)
But that was the best part of the whole thing.

VERA shakes her head after giving CLAY a look of incredulity.

                              VERA

    This is it, dear.

EXT   REAR OF VANDERCLEVEN'S HOUSE
A large brick fence encircles the backyard. VERA opens the gate and leads CLAY up to the back
steps. A basket sits just inside the back screen door. VERA takes the basket of clean clothes
and exchanges it for the basket of dirty.

                              CLAY
You mean you don't have to talk to anyone? You just pick up what they've left?

                              VERA
Yes, dear. The household servants are too busy running the house to take time to talk to
a washerwoman.

                              CLAY
                       (carries new basket)
What if something's stained and needs special treatment? My valet used to see to it that
the washerwoman knew stains needed to be removed or something needed to be sewn.

                              VERA
                   (reaches inside basket under covercloth
                       pulling out a sheet of paper)
See? Extra starch in the gentleman's shirts. And I'm to sew a new button on the young
miss' pinafore.

                              CLAY
Pinafore?

VERA

The little overdress girls wear to protect their real dresses?

CLAY

That has a name?

VERA

Everything has a name. Don't you read your bible? Adam named everything.

CLAY

Only the animals. I doubt Adam ever thought about women's clothing.

VERA

He might not have named them, but I bet he knew how to take them off.

They laugh as they go through the back gate and continue down the alley.

CLAY (CONT)

You never told me how you got started as a washerwoman. Or as a...lady of the evening, either.

VERA

Well, dear. One takes a recommendation from someone trustworthy, the other takes pluck.

EXT   LOWER CLASS HOUSING AREA   AFTERNOON
CLAY and VERA each carry a basket of dirties. CLAY observes the surroundings closely, never having really visited this part of Boston before. VERA is brisk and business-like as she strides down the street, occasionally greeting neighbors.

NEIGHBORWOMAN
(Swedish; leaning over a fence gossiping)
I see you're bringing them home with you now, Vera.

VERA

It's not like you're thinking, Edna. He's just a...friend.

NEIGHBORMAN
(Irish; smoking a pipe on steps)
So, that's what you call them now, eh? Friends is it?

VERA

Ignore them, Clay. They've nothing better to do.

CLAY follows VERA up the steps of a rundown brownstone, stopping to admire some of the stonework above the entry.

CLAY

These buildings must have been quite striking in their day.

VERA

Weren't we all?

INT   HALLWAY OF BROWNSTONE

VERA leads CLAY through the building, past playing children and a pair of arguing women, to the backyard.

EXT BACKYARD OF BROWNSTONE
Other women are already washing clothes in their own tubs with their own washboards. A high wooden fence surrounds the yard. A fire is situated dead center, where water boils for washing. The clothesline dominates the yard and is already covered with drying clothing. Several women greet VERA.

> FIRST WOMAN
> (Irish)
> 'Bout time you got here, Vera. You've only got so much daylight left, you know.

> VERA
> (sarcastically)
> Yes, dear, I know.
> (cheerfully to all present, VERA Cont.)
> I brought help with me today.

CLAY sets his basket down beside VERA's, then bows graciously to the women's hoots and cheers.

> CLAY
> At your service, ladies.

> SECOND WOMAN
> (German)
> Our service? That's a switch, eh, girls?

> VERA
> (to Clay)
> Oh, no you don't. You're mine.
> (to the women)
> The rest of you can get your own.

Laughter. CLAY helps VERA empty the basket she carried, learning to sort clothes for washing. He holds a small petticoat up to his front. The women laugh harder.

> FIRST WOMAN
> (tossing him another)
> Here, deary. Try this one. It's more your size.

CLAY holds the full-length petticoat up to himself. It's large, so he tries it on over his shirt and pants. It fits baggily.

> VERA
> It's you, dear.
> (pulls it tighter from back)
> But now it looks even better. Don't you think so, ladies?

The women cheer; some holler cat calls. CLAY strokes his five-o'clock-shadow, looks down at himself, and smiles.

INT CLAY'S HOTEL ROOM EVENING
CLAY, who already appears closely shaven, lathers up his face and prepares to shave again.
VERA, dressed in her prostitute outfit again, is laying out clothes on his bed.

> VERA
> I was able to pinch this dress from Mizz O'Neill's basket. I never liked her much, so I
> don't rightly mind if she gets in a bit of trouble for it.

> CLAY
> What will they do to her?

> VERA
> Oh, just dock the cost from her pay, I reckon. Or charge her with theft and throw her in
> jail.

> CLAY
> Jail? I can't let a woman go to jail just so I can have a dress to wear.

> VERA
> I don't see why not. She'll get three meals there, and lord knows she needs some regular
> eatin', what with being pregnant and all.

> CLAY
> She's pregnant?!

> VERA
> (deliberately dense)
> Don't you worry, dear. It'll never happen to you.

CLAY finishes shaving. VERA helps him dress, piece by piece. Then she sits him in the chair,
covers his clothes with a cloth, tucking it in at the chin. She begins to apply makeup, first a
heavy base coating of something like grease paint, which she dusts liberally with powder. Then
she has CLAY close his eyes, so she can apply eye liner and handmade fake eyelashes. She
rouges his cheeks and applies lipstick, finishing everything off with a wig.

> CLAY
> (indicating wig)
> Where did you get this?

> VERA
> A woman I know dresses corpses for burial. Apparently, someone didn't need this
> anymore.

INT LOBBY TO HOTEL NIGHT
CLAY, dressed as a woman, peers down into the small, poorly lit lobby from the upper landing
of the staircase. VERA peeks around him. The NIGHT CLERK sits at a smaller desk behind a
large, worn and dingy desk upon which sits a tattered register and a handbell. The CLERK is
clearly inebriated--his head is resting precariously on his hand, elbow resting on his little desk.
An almost empty glass sits tucked into one of the handy pigeonholes lining the back wall.

CLAY quietly descends the stairs with VERA right beside him. VERA giggles as they pass the
CLERK, who raises his head as though in fuzzy inquiry, then, seeing two women depart,
promptly tries to get comfortable again. An ELDERLY BLACK MAN is sweeping toward the

back of the hallway, just past the stairs. He stops sweeping long enough to watch the two "women" leave. He smiles and shakes his head before he resumes sweeping.

EXT REDLIGHT DISTRICT NIGHT
CLAY, still dressed as a woman, walks with VERA along the sidewalk. While his makeup is heavier, he's dressed much more modestly than VERA and the contrast seems to gather more attention.

                          MAN
                  (tips his hat politely)
    Ladies. I couldn't help noticing two such lovely creatures as you are. I was wondering...

                          VERA
    We're not interested tonight.

                          MAN
    I was only wondering if...

                          VERA
    I told you; we're not interested.

CLAY smiles, unsure what to say. The MAN takes the smile as an invitation.

                          MAN
    Perhaps you're not interested, ma'am, but this young lady seems to be.
                  (offers elbow)
    Care to take a stroll with me, sweetheart?

                          CLAY
                  (his voice is noticeably deep)
    No, thank you.

The MAN is startled. Looks CLAY over carefully, then leaves hastily. VERA and CLAY laugh.

                          VERA
    You nearly scared the poor man to death.

                          CLAY
                  (mock feminine voice)
    Pity that.

INT WOMEN'S CLOTHING STORE MORNING
CLAY, dressed as a woman, is looking at readymade dresses. A SALESMAN waits on him.

                          CLAY
                  (in a more believable feminine voice)
    I'm really looking for something more elegant, but modestly priced. It's my first
    time...to go to the opera, you see. And I don't want to stand out too much.

The SALESMAN shows him several pastel colored dresses. He chooses one.

                          SALESMAN
    We'll have to make alterations, of course, ma'am. Would you care to step this way and
    Mrs. Noonagan will take your measurements.

                          CLAY
                  (hands him a slip of paper)
That's not necessary. My...seamstress uses these measurements.

                        SALESMAN
                   (slightly offended)
I'm sure they would do for her, ma'am, but we sell only quality work here and we'd be
able to make a much better fit if you'll allow us to take your measurements ourselves.
I'm sure you understand.

                          CLAY
I do, I assure you. But you see I'm in rather a hurry. And I'm sure your highly skilled
seamstress or tailor will do an excellent job with these figures. When will the dress be
done?

                        SALESMAN
By four this afternoon, ma'am. But...

                          CLAY
That will be fine. Thank you.

INT CLAY'S HOTEL ROOM LATE AFTERNOON
CLAY is shaving again. VERA lounges on the bed, which is partially covered with CLAY's new
dress.

                          VERA
I hope you know what you're doing.

                          CLAY
I know.

                          VERA
You know what they'll do to you, if they find out.

                          CLAY
What can they do to me?

                          VERA
Brand you a witch. Tar and feather you. Cut off your...

                          CLAY
Nonsense. Many of the boys in the Army dressed like girls for dances.

                          VERA
That's because they were short on real women. There's no shortage here, dear.

                          CLAY
                    (finishes shaving)
This is the last opera of the season. I have to go. I have to know if I am convincing.

                          VERA
Why? Do you want to be a woman the rest of your life?

CLAY
The idea has its appeal. Being a woman's not all bad, you know.

VERA
(standing up)
Not when you have a choice. If you're determined to do this pigheaded thing, let's finish it up then.

CLAY undresses and VERA starts to dress him.

VERA
It's really too bad.

CLAY
What?

VERA
(stroking his bare chest)
That this must be wasted.

(kisses him passionately)

CLAY
(pushing her firmly back)
Vera!
(more gently, holding her hands)
I love you, Vera. But not like that.

A pained look crosses VERA's face, but she continues helping CLAY dress by telling him what to do, trying not to touch him unless it's necessary. This time, she instructs him on how to apply the makeup, instead of doing it herself, taking care to stay back, touching him as little as possible.

EXT BOSTON OPERA HOUSE A WARM SPRING EVENING
CLAY, dressed as a woman (more convincingly than ever before), descends from a cab. He stops to look at the people milling about before ascending the steps, carefully pulling up his dress as he steps. People notice the solitary woman, but aren't shocked, assuming she'll join a party. The longer CLAY dons his feminine self, the more convincing he becomes as the film progresses. Eventually, he should need little makeup or other conveyances to appear feminine.

INT ENTRYWAY TO OPERA HOUSE
Flowers adorn the entryway. CLAY stops to smell some, plucking a bloom to carry. As he smells it, he examines the people in the room to notice reactions. He smiles at those who meet his gaze. He purchases a ticket for the only class of seating available.

INT OPERA THEATER SAME NIGHT
A MAN stands to let CLAY in to his seat in the general seating on the floor. CLAY uses opera glasses to view the occupants of the boxes above, looking for friends. He spies CHARLES and TILLY who don't even seem to be communicating, although TILLY is aware of CHARLES' presence. CLAY lends his glasses to the MAN next to him, who smiles congenially at him, obviously looking him over--convinced he's a woman. Music starts and the lighting is dimmed.

INT OPERA LOBBY SAME NIGHT
Intermission. People are buying ice cream in a cup or glasses of champagne. CLAY watches for CHARLES and TILLY. Once he spots them, he maneuvers his way to be near them. TILLY

notices him observing them, and assumes "she" is ogling CHARLES, so steps between them, blocking CLAY's view. CLAY maneuvers again, watching CHARLES, who is chatting with cronies, closely. CLAY, not watching where he's going, bumps into TILLY, causing her to spill her champagne. Everyone watches.

CLAY
(patting at her dress)

I'm so sorry, miss.

TILLY
(accusingly)

You...

(remembering her manners)

It's...all right. I think I can get it clean. I'll just visit the powder room. Maybe one of the matrons can help me.

As TILLY moves off, CLAY looks up to meet CHARLES' eyes. CHARLES stares for several seconds, and CLAY begins to shift expectantly, hoping for but fearing detection. Finally, CHARLES looks away and resumes his conversation.

EXT OPERA HOUSE LATER THAT NIGHT
CLAY follows CHARLES and TILLY out, motioning the ATTENDANT to hail a cab. He has his DRIVER follow their carriage at a discreet distance.

EXT OSGOOD RESIDENCE SAME NIGHT
CLAY has driver stop the cab at the corner, where he can still see CHARLES and TILLY as CHARLES sees her to the door. When they embrace, CLAY leans forward as if to see better.

EXT STALLARD MANSION SAME NIGHT
Again, CLAY has the DRIVER stop a distance away. CHARLES' driver steers the carriage into the circular driveway, lets him off at the door, then drives around back. CHARLES looks around, even in the direction of the street where CLAY's carriage is parked, then disappears inside. CLAY sighs, then orders the driver on.

INT CLAY'S HOTEL ROOM NEXT DAY
CLAY lays across the bed. VERA sits in the window sill.

VERA

Why didn't you introduce yourself?

CLAY

I didn't know what to say.

VERA
(sarcastically)

There's always, "Hello, how are you, won't you please fuck me?"

Their eyes meet. Both glare angrily.

CLAY

You don't understand, Vera.

Stop telling me I don't understand. I've seen lust hundreds of times, Mister Wright. I think you should forget him.

CLAY
I don't have much choice, do I?

MONTAGE:
EXT   BUSY STREET   MORNING
It's the beginning of summer. CLAY, dressed as a washerwoman (makeup is still noticeable), carries a basket of clothes.

EXT   ALLEYWAY   SAME MORNING
CLAY dodges other delivery people as he makes his way to a particular back yard. He enters the gate, trades baskets, and exits, heading back the way he came.

EXT   WASHWOMEN'S YARD (VERA'S)   LATE AFTERNOON
In the same backyard as before, CLAY scrubs clothes on a washboard in a washtub near VERA, who does the same. He joins the chatter occasionally but is beginning to look tired and haggard.

EXT   PARK THEATER   AFTERNOON
A comic theater production plays out on a stage in the middle of the park. Mostly lower & lower middle class people watch, laugh, and talk among themselves. CLAY, whose hair is noticeably longer, is dressed as a man and sits on a blanket on the grass next to VERA, who looks at him longingly. He seems more relaxed, but also preoccupied.

EXT   OUTSIDE MARKET   DAY
VERA & CLAY, dressed as a woman, shop for groceries. She picks up a pomegranate and teases him visibly about its sexual symbolism. People begin to watch while they also try to appear oblivious.

INT   A CATHOLIC CHURCH   MORNING
VERA & CLAY, dressed as a woman in her Sunday best, enter. VERA dips holy water before walking down the aisle. CLAY follows. VERA kneels on one knee quickly and crosses herself before entering a pew. CLAY follows.

EXT   FRONT OF VERA'S APARTMENT BUILDING   EVENING
On the large sidewalk and the steps in front, VERA and CLAY, as a man, share lemonade and chat with the neighbors, washerwomen, and working class men. One of the men pours beer from his own glass mug into CLAY's lemonade (a shandy). Intrigued, CLAY sips it, likes it and everyone laughs. Children run up and down the street, playing baseball in its earlier form.

EXT   VERA'S BACKYARD   LATE AFTERNOON
It's now the height of summer. The women's sleeves are rolled as high as they can get them. Some have fastened their skirts up. Few are actually washing; most lounge in the shade drinking shandies (lemonade and beer). Fewer clothes cover the lines.

INT   CLAY'S HOTEL ROOM   NIGHT
Finished shaving his beard, CLAY begins to shave his legs. He sets the washbasin on the floor and uses his shaving brush to stroke the suds up and down his calf. Black net stockings lie in a pile on the floor next to him.

EXT VERA'S BACKYARD EARLY AFTERNOON
CLAY enters, his basket not as full as usual (the rich are out of town on vacation). He makes an elaborate point of rolling up his sleeves (his arms aren't noticeably hairy anyway), and pinning up his skirt before he pours heated water into his tub. VERA points and jokes about his now hairless legs. CLAY throws cold water from a pitcher on her.

EXT VERA'S BACKYARD EARLY EVENING
The clothesline, which crisscrosses the yard from wooden fence to wooden fence, is empty. Most of the women are gone. VERA and CLAY lounge on the steps, sipping shandies.

                              VERA
     It starts soon, doesn't it?

                              CLAY
     The first ball is next month.

                              VERA
     Must be nice to be rich enough to leave town when it's hot and come back to all the
     excitement of the social season.

                              CLAY
     Yes, it was.

                              VERA
     You'll be going back, then?

                              CLAY
     Yes.

                              VERA
     Why do you need those people so much? Why can't you just go on as you have been?

CLAY doesn't respond. He finishes his shandy, unpins his skirt, which falls around his legs as he stands. He runs his hands through his own hair, which is now long enough that he doesn't have to wear a wig. He looks around the yard, then at VERA who hasn't moved. Their eyes meet. She turns away, saddened. He picks up his basket and mounts the steps. Vera leans aside, letting him pass.

INT BALLROOM NIGHT
The room is filled almost to capacity. The August heat and the heat of bodies combine. All the women fan themselves, with the men standing near windows and doorways for relief. Many escape outside onto balconies, several of which line one side of the room.

CLAY, dressed as a woman, dances with successive men. At first, he mistakes the proper stance, trying to smile his way through his errors. Eventually, he develops a kind of rhythm, and obviously begins to enjoy himself.

JOHN PAYNE, dressed in a cavalry uniform, enters, looks around, and joins some young men he knows to one side of the room. Eventually, he dances with successive women. Offering to get his current partner, TILLY, a cup of punch, he returns to discover she's talking with CLAY and CHARLES. JOHN is intrigued when this "woman" quickly persuades CHARLES to dance. JOHN watches enviously, noticing the strange quality of the attraction between the two--as though CHARLES is at once attracted and repelled by CLAY. After the dance, CLAY seeks out dance partners continuously, attempting to avoid JOHN. CLAY steps out onto an empty balcony to cool off. JOHN quickly follows.

EXT SMALL STONE BALCONY NIGHT
The view overlooks a park. Lights flicker like fireflies amongst the trees. A faint breeze ruffles CLAY's dress. Because he's sweating, his makeup is glossy and obviously heavy, so he powders his nose to try to take off the shine. JOHN pauses at the doorway, observing CLAY who faces the park, before stepping up behind him.

                    JOHN
     It's not much cooler out here, is it?

                    CLAY
                 (startled, cornered)
     No, it's not.

JOHN moves over to the other corner of the balcony. They seem to square off like boxers. CLAY is worried about his makeup melting off, but doesn't dare touch his face because it will rub off on his gloves. He looks toward doorway, picks up his skirts as though about to leave, then drops them, fanning himself instead.

                    JOHN
     I don't remember seeing you before. And I used to come to these things often, just after the war.
                 (extends his hand, not moving)
     I'm Lieutenant John Gordon Payne. And you are?

CLAY declines the handshake, covering his face even more with his fan.

                    CLAY
     Shouldn't we be properly introduced?

                    JOHN
     You are absolutely right. I beg your pardon, ma'am. I'll find someone to introduce us properly.

JOHN disappears inside. CLAY turns back toward the park. He's obviously agitated, alternately opening his fan, waving it and clicking it shut. JOHN quickly returns with TILLY.

                    TILLY
     Oh my, it's much cooler out here, isn't it?

                    JOHN
     Almost chilly.

TILLY moves over beside CLAY. JOHN steps up close to CLAY's other side. CLAY steps back, as though to leave, but JOHN puts his hand on CLAY's arm.

                    JOHN
     Tilly, I've been trying to strike up a conversation with this charming young lady, but she insists on being properly introduced first.

JOHN releases his touch. CLAY dabs his face carefully with a powderpuff. TILLY smiles, watching the interaction between the two with curiosity.

                              TILLY
You two don't know each other? I could have sworn...by the way you two...

                              CLAY
                         (unsteadily)
No, dear, I've never met this man before in my life.

                              TILLY
                          (skeptical)
John, may I have the pleasure of introducing you to Emma Bovary.
                     (whispers to John)
She's a divorcee from New York, you know.

                              JOHN
                       (bowing slightly)
How do you do, Miss...Bovary, is it?

                              TILLY
Isn't that exciting? Just like the woman in the novel.

                              JOHN
Yes, quite a coincidence, isn't it?

                              CLAY
                          (to Tilly)
And...?

                              TILLY
Oh, yes. Emma, this is Lieutenant John G. Payne of the United States Cavalry. He's killed almost as many Indians as Custer.

                              CLAY
               (gently taking John's extended hand)
How...intriguing.
                          (pauses)
Come to think of it, I have heard of you, Lt. Payne. I understand you're quite a lady killer, too.

                              TILLY
                     (compulsorily shocked)
Emma.

                              JOHN
                      (feigning innocence)
I assure you, Miss Bovary, your reputation is safe with me.
                    (JOHN extends his elbow)
Shall we dance? If you'll excuse us, Miss Osgood.

CLAY takes JOHN's arm with feigned reluctance, and they disappear through the doorway.

INT BALLROOM SAME NIGHT
JOHN and CLAY waltz to the Nutcracker Suite by Tchaikovsky.

> JOHN
>
> You'll excuse me if I sound practiced, but...I feel as though I've met you somewhere before.

> CLAY
> (coquetishly)
>
> Perhaps you have, Lt. Payne.

> JOHN
> (smiling conspiratorily)
>
> And were we...friends?

CLAY teases him with a smile as they continue to dance.

INT REFRESHMENT ROOM SAME NIGHT
JOHN brings CLAY, who is sitting on a couch, a glass of champagne. They strike cheers daintily. They continue to sit and drink and talk, gradually getting closer together and more relaxed with each other. Other couples come and go. Soon the room is mostly empty with just the two of them and another couple who sits across from each other in chairs closely drawn together on the other side of the room. JOHN sits down with yet another glass of champagne. CLAY tries to wave it off.

> CLAY
> (his voice deeper, tipsy)
>
> No, no, no. I don't want any more.

> JOHN
> (more sober)
>
> You know. I think I like you even more when you're drunk.

> CLAY
>
> I am not drunk.

> JOHN
>
> Maybe you should be.

INT CLAY'S HOTEL ROOM LATE NEXT MORNING
Light streams through the unshaded window. It's late enough that the sunlight angles in and touches the end of the bed, hitting CLAY in the face as he lies prostrate across the bed. He still has makeup on, but it is messy. There is a lump in the bed beside him, but it's not evident that it's another person until CLAY sits up and takes stock of the room and himself. Once he realizes someone is there, he looks down at himself, realizing he's nude and tries to cover himself up. In doing so, he pulls the sheet off JOHN, who remains asleep. Carefully, he slips out of bed, stepping over to the mirror to examine his makeup. He obviously has a hangover. He pulls on the corset, as though for protection, and hastily, but quietly, wipes off the old makeup, shaves and begins applying new. He's almost finished, when he realizes John is awake and lying on his side on the bed, watching him.

> JOHN
>
> Good morning, Madame Bovary. Or should I say, Mr. Wright?

                              CLAY
                           (horrified)
You know?

                              JOHN
How could I not know? Or don't you remember last night?

                              CLAY
Last night? You mean the ball?

                              JOHN
                           (laughing)
I believe there was more than one.

JOHN stands and crosses, nude, to stand behind CLAY, who still stands in front of the mirror.
They look at each other in the mirror.

                              JOHN
Or do you do this sort of thing only when you're drunk?

                              CLAY
This sort of thing? You mean wear women's clothes?

                              JOHN
                   (pressing himself against Clay)
No, this sort of thing.

                              CLAY
Oh.

JOHN smiles so that CLAY, finally, smiles back. JOHN swats CLAY on the behind as he moves
away to pull on his pants.

                              JOHN
I knew there was something about you I remembered. But it's been a long time since
grammar school.

                              CLAY
Yes, I've changed a lot since then. Although I was still afraid you'd recognize me.

                              JOHN
                           (laughs)
Actually, I probably would never have been able to remember who you were, if you
hadn't told me.

                              CLAY
                        (rubbing his head)
I told you?

                              JOHN
I believe you mentioned it after the tenth glass of champagne. Of course, it was already
obvious by then that you were no miss.

                                    CLAY
What do you mean?

                                    JOHN
The deeper you sink into the bottle, the deeper your voice gets.

By now, JOHN is nearly fully dressed. CLAY has been watching him in the mirror.

                               JOHN (CONT)
So, did you mean what you said last night?

CLAY stops applying makeup, turning to look at JOHN.

                                    CLAY
Which part? I haven't the faintest idea what I said, to be honest.

JOHN stands, pants not completely fastened and crosses over to CLAY again, touching the makeup on his face, rubbing the greasy stuff on his fingers and smelling it. He smiles.

                                    JOHN
You said you wanted to fuck the president.

CLAY resumes applying the makeup.

                                    CLAY
Are you sure I didn't say he was fucked?

JOHN crosses to window and looks out, sitting on sill.

                                    JOHN
Maybe you did. I remember now something about his Indian policy, how you thought he should be held accountable for the buffalo? Or something like that.

CLAY finishes and turns to look at JOHN. He takes on decidedly feminine mannerisms and a convincing female voice

                                    CLAY
You're the first man who's paid attention when a woman talked politics.

JOHN stands and crosses to CLAY, inspecting the whole effect carefully.

                                    JOHN
So you really consider yourself a woman now?

CLAY smiles smugly and traces a hand down one of JOHN's arms coquettishly.

                                    CLAY
I've discovered, my dear Lt. Payne, that I can be anyone I want to be--Emma Bovary or Claypool Wright.

                                    JOHN
                                 (grimacing)
You've got to pitch that Emma Bovary as a name. Don't people see right through that?

                                    CLAY
          I admit I thought of the name on the spur of the moment, but I discovered something
          about humanity, old chum. People want to believe you. It's either that, or they want to
          be fooled.

JOHN sits on the bed, clearly inviting CLAY to join him.

                                    JOHN
          Or they are fools. Same difference.

CLAY sits on the bed next to JOHN. They lean close together, clearly toying with intimacy.
CLAY still speaks in a feminine voice.

                                    CLAY
          What about you? When did you start....

                                    JOHN
          Fucking men?

                                    CLAY
          I would have put it more delicately.

                                    JOHN
          What's delicate about it?

JOHN caresses CLAY. CLAY responds. They begin undressing each other.
MONTAGE:
INT CLAY'S HOTEL ROOM NIGHT
Lights from the street expose the room. CLAY and JOHN are asleep in the bed, lying in each
other's arms. Perspiration stands out freshly on their faces.

INT CLAY'S HOTEL ROOM MORNING
JOHN is helping CLAY dress, tightening his corset for him.

EXT A SHOPPING DISTRICT DAY
JOHN and CLAY, as a woman, are window shopping. JOHN drags CLAY into a shop and they
emerge with a new hat for CLAY.

INT A BAR EVENING
JOHN and CLAY, dressed as a man, are drinking with JOHN's military cronies. They laugh and
joke with the others. They look at each other significantly, smiling as though enjoying their
secret.

INT CLAY'S HOTEL ROOM MORNING
Sunlight coats the bed where JOHN and CLAY are making love.

EXT RESIDENTIAL STREET MORNING
JOHN accompanies CLAY, dressed as a washerwoman, on his rounds. CLAY carries the basket.
JOHN seems bored.

EXT VERA'S BACKYARD AFTERNOON
CLAY and JOHN appear at back door and head toward CLAY's washtub. The jovial
atmosphere, as the women realize the serious nature of their relationship, changes as their

support swings to VERA. VERA tries not to show her hurt feelings but fails. CLAY and JOHN joke, seemingly oblivious to the women's attitudes. The women begin to leave.

                              CLAY
John, this is my good friend, Vera. She helped me become the woman I am today. Vera, this is my schoolboy chum, Lt. John Payne.

                              VERA
Lieutenant.

                              JOHN
Dear Vera. Clay's mentioned you often in the last couple of days. Believe me, I'll be eternally grateful for what you've done for this young man.

                              VERA
You mean woman, don't you?

                              JOHN
Man, woman, what's the difference?

                              VERA
Considerable. You know a man's out to get you, but I used to think I could trust a woman.

                              CLAY
And when someone contains the spirits of both?

                              VERA
I'd say one of them needs to be exorcised.

CLAY and JOHN look at each other. VERA leaves.

EXT A PARK AFTERNOON
Leaves are changing color and the wind is brisk. The sound of rustling leaves mixes with the sounds of the city.

JOHN and Clay, dressed as a woman, sit on an isolated bench. Clay's long hair and dress whip in the wind, distracting him. JOHN takes his hand, but Clay pulls it away to push his hair from his face.

                              JOHN
What's left for you here?

                              CLAY
My friends, my family.

                              JOHN
Your friends don't want to be associated with a suspected homosexual. And your family has disowned you.

                              CLAY
What's out West? How would I make a living? What if you decide you'd rather be married to someone else? Or worse, what if you get killed in some Indian battle? What do I do if the Indians attack?

JOHN

I thought you were the one who wants the president to see them as human beings, not savages?

CLAY

They still kill people from time to time.

JOHN

I know. I've seen the aftermath.

CLAY

People like us aren't supposed to marry. No one would ever let us.

JOHN

I've yet to hear of anyone lifting a woman's skirt to see if she's a she before they'd let her take the vows.

CLAY looks searchingly at JOHN, who smiles and takes CLAY's hand, kissing the back of it.

INT JUSTICE OF THE PEACE'S RESIDENCE EVENING
CLAY, in the nicest dress he owns, stands next to JOHN as they exchange vows in front of the justice. Two witnesses stand to one side--the JUSTICE'S WIFE and THEIR MAID. JOHN smiles broadly before he kisses CLAY. The JUSTICE insists on his turn.

INT A PASSENGER CAR ON A TRAIN DAY
CLAY, now ELEANOR PAYNE, sits next to JOHN, who dozes. ELEANOR watches the women with their children, the businessmen reading their newspapers, etc. She opens a cloth package on her lap, taking out a sandwich wrapped in waxed paper. She unwraps and eats it as she turns to watch the terrain pass.

INT SAME TRAIN EVENING
ELEANOR sleeps against JOHN as JOHN cleans his pistol. Two other men, a businessman and an American Indian dressed in a suit with a turban, sit across from them. The Indian watches JOHN clean his gun. The businessman watches the Indian.

INT ANOTHER TRAIN DAY
Less plush than the earlier train, the coach is spartan and dirtier. The seats are wooden, not cushioned. ELEANOR and JOHN eat apples from the cloth bag. The conductor comes through announcing Manhattan, Kansas. ELEANOR looks nervously outside. JOHN checks his pocket watch.

EXT MANHATTAN DEPOT DAY
JOHN deposits ELEANOR on a bench next to their luggage. He motions for her to wait. ELEANOR checks her makeup, discreetly, in a hand mirror. A man and a woman pass by as they go to the ticket counter. The man doffs his hat and smiles. The woman pulls him onward. ELEANOR smiles. As she looks around, observing the town, she sees a large building with a steeple sitting on the most prominent hill in the immediate area--the beginnings of Kansas State University.

EXT FLINT HILLS DAY
ELEANOR and JOHN ride horseback. ELEANOR is sidesaddle. JOHN leads a mule which carries their luggage. ELEANOR looks around anxiously.

ELEANOR
Wasn't there any other route to the fort? Are you sure we won't be attacked by Indians?

JOHN
The nearest Indian's probably in the Dakota or Oklahoma territories. We're more likely to be attacked by bandits.

ELEANOR
Bandits? You never mentioned anything about bandits.

JOHN
I guess it slipped my mind.

Their horses head up a gravelly grade. Train tracks run along the top of the ridge. ELEANOR stops her horse and stares, incredulous, at the rails.

ELEANOR
A train? A train runs through here? Does it go to Fort Riley?

JOHN pulls his horse to a halt after he's made it down the other side of the ridge and turns to look back.

ELEANOR (CONT)
Why didn't we take the train?

JOHN
(patting horse's neck)
I had to pick up Cochise at the stable where I left him before I went on leave.

ELEANOR
Your horse? I'm sitting sidesaddle, twisting the hell out of my back, because you had to pick up your horse?

JOHN
Good, Clay...I mean, Eleanor. You've got it down.

ELEANOR
Got what down?

JOHN
Being a woman.

JOHN whoops and kicks his horse into a fast gate, pulling the mule along, too, suitcases banging its sides, trunk swaying on top. ELEANOR grimaces and urges her horse down the grade.

EXT FORT RILEY EVENING
ELEANOR sits sidesaddle as she waits for JOHN to come out of a large limestone building. JOHN's horse and mule are tied up to the hitching post. A train whistles in the near distance. Soldiers of various ethnic backgrounds, including an occasional Indian scout, come and go out of the building occasionally; most smile and nod their heads toward ELEANOR. Other limestone buildings dot the grounds, with dirt roads crisscrossing the green grass. A company of black soldiers drills under the command of a white officer on a parade ground in the distance.

A very young soldier (HIGGINS, about 16 years old) comes out of the building and approaches ELEANOR, saluting.

                                HIGGINS
                         (Australian accent)
Mrs. Payne, ma'am. I'm Private Higgins. I've been instructed to escort you to your new quarters, ma'am.

                                ELEANOR
What about John...I mean, Lt. Payne? Isn't he coming?

                                HIGGINS
Presently, ma'am. He's got business to attend to. He says he'll be along shortly and that I'm to see to your needs until he arrives.

HIGGINS unties the mule and grasps ELEANOR's horse's reins. He signals for a private to take COCHISE.

                                ELEANOR
My needs? Where is he taking Cochise?

                                HIGGINS
Cochise, ma'am?

                                ELEANOR
Lt. Payne's horse.

                                HIGGINS
To the officers' stable, ma'am. Don't worry. He'll see to the horse's needs.

                                ELEANOR
Well, as long as everyone's needs are attended to.

EXT A LIMESTONE TOWNHOUSE DUSK
HIGGINS helps ELEANOR dismount and leads her up the steps to the entrance on the left. He opens the door for her and escorts her in.

INT THE HALLWAY OF THE TOWNHOUSE
HIGGINS lights several lamps, as ELEANOR removes her hat and looks around.

                                HIGGINS
This here's the parlor. Over here's the sitting room, and through there is the kitchen. The bedrooms are upstairs.

The rooms are already furnished, although sparingly. No pictures hang on the wall, but a mirror does hang near the doorway. ELEANOR inspects herself and begins to smile.

                             HIGGINS (CONT)
And there's a pump in the kitchen, so you don't need to draw water. You share the outhouse, of course, with the couple who live next door, if you'll pardon my bluntness, ma'am.

                          ELEANOR
There's a couple living next door?

                          HIGGINS
Yes, ma'am. These are the married officers' quarters.

                          ELEANOR
And where do you live, Pvt. Higgins?

                          HIGGINS
In the barracks on the other side of the parade grounds, ma'am.

                          ELEANOR
                    (extending her hand)
Please, call me Eleanor.

                          HIGGINS
Oh, I couldn't do that, ma'am.
                    (heading toward door)
I'll unpack the mule and bring in your things, ma'am. Just let me know what goes where
and I'll put things away, too, if you'd like.

                          ELEANOR
Thank you, but I'm sure that won't be necessary.

ELEANOR runs a hand along the banister as she starts upstairs. She gets to the top and
realizes she needs light. Returning downstairs, she finds a hurricane lamp on the side table
next to the entrance, lights it off one of the lamps on the wall, and returns to the stairs.
Meanwhile, HIGGINS brings the luggage in and sets it near the stairs.

                          HIGGINS
If that's all, ma'am, I'll go over to the mess hall and bring you back something to eat.

                          ELEANOR
That's not necessary, private.

                          HIGGINS
Captain's orders, ma'am.

                          ELEANOR
Captain? Captain who?

                          HIGGINS
Captain Payne, ma'am. He was promoted in his absence, ma'am. He told me he
especially wanted me to see to it you got fed.

                          ELEANOR
                    (pleased)
Really? Does that sort of thing happen often?

                          HIGGINS
Well, usually the officers' wives cook their own food, but seeings how you don't have any
food stocked up yet...

ELEANOR

No. I mean Lt....Captain Payne's promotion.

I thought most of the regular Army commissions were demoted after the war since the Army reduced the number of troops.

HIGGINS

It was, ma'am. Only, out here, sometimes there's need of a successor.

ELEANOR

A successor?

HIGGINS

Yes, ma'am. Captain Fredericks was killed on patrol while Lieutenant, I mean Captain, Payne was gone, ma'am. The Colonel needed a man to fill his boots, and Capt. Payne was the best choice, so I'm told, ma'am. Now, if you don't need me for a few minutes, I'll get your dinner.

HIGGINS leaves. ELEANOR stands holding the lamp for a few moments, then heads back upstairs.

INT   UPSTAIRS BEDROOM   NIGHT
ELEANOR places the lamp on the nightstand after lighting the lamp on the wall. She sits on the edge of the mattress and tests it out.

ELEANOR
(to herself)

I wonder if this was Captain Fredericks' bed.

FEMALE VOICE (OS)
(Spanish accent)

No, it wasn't.

ELEANOR jumps up, startled. She turns to face the door, where a shadowy figure stands.

ELEANOR

Who are you?

MARIA STRAW, a plump young woman (Mexican-American, Chicana), enters laughing.

MARIA

I'm sorry. I didn't mean to startle you.
(Rushes forward, hand outstretched)
I'm Maria Straw, Captain Benjamin Straw's wife. I live next door. I came over to be hospitable and to see if you need any help moving in. I knocked, but I guess you didn't hear me.

ELEANOR
(recovering)

No, I didn't.
(taking MARIA's handshake)
I'm Eleanor Payne. Wife of Lieutenant...I mean, Captain Payne. It seems I just got used to calling him one thing and now he's something else.

MARIA

You'll get used to it. Promotions happened fast during the war. They're not quite as fast out here, but there always seems to be someone filling a gap somewhere.

ELEANOR
(needing to do something)
Where are my manners? I should offer you...something...shouldn't I?

MARIA

Not when you first move in, dear. It's my obligation to offer you something--as a housewarming gift, so to speak. I brought a peach cobbler. It's downstairs on your dining table.

ELEANOR
(not used to such familiarity so quickly)
Really? How...thoughtful of you.

MARIA

We can boil a pot of tea, help ourselves to some cobbler, and chat while we wait for the men to return.

ELEANOR

Return?

INT KITCHEN SAME NIGHT
MARIA sticks wood in the stove, under the burner, and lights it.

ELEANOR sits at the table, while MARIA bustles about making tea, cutting cobbler and serving both up after she wipes down the dusty table with water from the pump. MARIA chatters while she works.

MARIA

Yes, the Army wasn't meant for wives. They never give us a second thought. If they need the men for something, well, they take them, no "thank you, ma'am"s for the lending of your husband, either. No, when you marry a man in the Army, you might as well accept the fact you've married the Army.

MARIA sprinkles tea leaves in china cups and pours in the hot water. She sets the teapot on a trivet, and puts a cosy over it to keep the water warm.

ELEANOR

Really?

MARIA

Yes. I always thought the hardest thing would be sharing my husband with other women, if he saw fit, but I believe it's a thousand times worse to share him with the Army.

ELEANOR

I see.

MARIA
(patting ELEANOR's hand)
Don't worry, amiga. We'll manage. Why, the last woman who lived here got on real well with me. She loved to cook and I...(laughs) love to eat.

ELEANOR
So, that's all you did? Cook and eat?

MARIA
Dios, no. We did lots of things. Why there are two towns, Manhattan and Junction City within riding distance for shopping. And there's the monthly officers' ball at the officers' club. Well, really it's just a dance, but they like to think it's a ball. We officers wives take turns planning them and serving the refreshments.

MARIA (CONT)
(serves the cobbler)
There's a lot to keep us busy.

There's a knock on the front door. ELEANOR jumps, startled. MARIA laughs, getting up to go answer it.

MARIA
Oh, that's probably Higgins back with your dinner from the mess hall.

ELEANOR takes the opportunity of MARIA's absence to look around the kitchen. She rubs her face, realizing stubble has grown into shadow. She gets a compact out of her purse and pats cake makeup on. After a vain attempt at coverup, she rolls her eyes and groans.

ELEANOR
I wonder if there are other hairy women in Kansas.

INT TOWNHOUSE MASTER BEDROOM MORNING
ELEANOR is in bed asleep. She's sleeping in a long cotton nightgown, which contrasts with her more apparent beard stubble. JOHN, dusty and haggard, enters the room carrying his boots. He quietly sets them next to the chifforobe. While looking around the room, impressed with what ELEANOR has already unpacked, yet noting the partially unpacked trunk, he begins stripping, pausing to pour water from the pitcher into the wash bowl on a stand near the doorway. He washes his face and arms, then finishes stripping, down to his shorts and undershirt. He tries to quietly crawl into bed next to ELEANOR, but she opens her eyes and smiles.

ELEANOR
You're back. Finally. I was so worried. What time is it?

JOHN
Just a little past eight.

ELEANOR
In the morning?

JOHN
Yes, dear. Now give me a kiss and let me get some sleep.

                                   ELEANOR
I don't even get an explanation? Where did you go? What did you do?

                                    JOHN
I was out with another woman.

                                   ELEANOR
                            (hitting him with a pillow)
Ha, ha. Where were you really?

                                    JOHN
Let me sleep until noon, then I'll fill you in on all the details of my honeymoon
adventures in Kansas.

ELEANOR gives JOHN an exasperated look. JOHN plays innocent and helpless, making
ELEANOR laugh. She kisses him, then slips out of bed. She pulls a dress and underthings out
of the chifforobe. She pours the water from the washbasin into the chamber pot and pours out
more for herself. She strips, with JOHN looking on appreciatively, down to camisole and
underpants. First, she inspects her chest hair.

                                   ELEANOR
I wish I didn't have to shave so much so often.

                                    JOHN
Your chest has never been very hairy, Clay.

                                   ELEANOR
Eleanor. You better get used to calling me that, or you'll slip up at the wrong moment
and give us away, you know.

                                    JOHN
                                (rolling over)
Yeah, yeah.

                                   ELEANOR
I wish there was some way to get rid of hair. I guess I should be glad I'm not going bald
yet.

                                    JOHN
Try pulling it out by the root.

                                   ELEANOR
You mean plucking it?
                                (thinks about it)
I have heard that some women use gauze and candle wax to get rid of their facial hair.

                                    JOHN
                             (muffled into pillow)
Sounds painful.

                                   ELEANOR
                                (shaving face)
That's what I thought.

ELEANOR, Cont.
(pause)
You know. It's really not fair that the Army can just send you off like that. Doesn't the
Army have any chivalry in its big bureaucratic heart?
(pause)
John?

ELEANOR turns to look at JOHN, who is snoring lightly. She smiles and returns to her
shaving.

INT TOWNHOUSE KITCHEN MORNING
ELEANOR is going through the cupboards, taking stock of pots and pans. The door which leads
into the backyard is open, with a screen door to keep out insects. The one window which faces
out back is open, too. There is a knock on the back screen door. ELEANOR looks out the
window.

ELEANOR
Maria. How good to see you. Please come in.

MARIA enters carrying a light wooden box of groceries.

MARIA
Good morning, Eleanor. I brought you a little housewarming gift.

ELEANOR
But you brought me one last night.

MARIA
Oh, that little cobbler? That was only something to fill your travel empty stomach. This
is much more practical. Baking supplies and goods for your larder.

ELEANOR
That's very generous of you. Thank you.

MARIA
(pleased with the reception)
De nada. You're welcome.
(helps ELEANOR put things away)
You know, Eleanor, I know I've only known you a short while, but I already feel as though
though I've known you forever. As though you're the sister I never had.

ELEANOR smiles tentatively, looking guiltily at the supplies in her hands before she continues
putting things away.

INT STRAWS' DINING ROOM EVENING
ELEANOR and JOHN sit across from each other at the dining table, with BEN and MARIA at
either end of the table. MARIA has gone all out on the meal, serving a roast, several vegetables,
mashed potatoes, gravy, several kinds of bread, all of which are spread on the fairly large table
between its occupants, so that the basket of wildflowers and two candles, the only light in the
room, seem crowded in the middle. BEN, a young, Black Irishman (which means he's Irish
with Spanish blood) who is already losing his hair, has a full dark beard and mustache, which
stand out against his pale face. In contrast to MARIA, he is tall and slender.

                              BEN
                      (swirling his wine)
Well, mother, you've outdone yourself again.

                            ELEANOR
                           (to Ben)
Mother?

                             JOHN
Yes, MARIA, these were quite sumptuous eats.

                            ELEANOR
                          (to MARIA)
Mother?

                             MARIA
                    (beaming at the praise)
I'm glad you enjoyed the meal.
                    (whispers to ELEANOR)
It's just a pet name he calls me. He says I remind him of his mother. Except, I think,
she was a better cook.

                             JOHN
Aren't mothers always?

                            ELEANOR
You've never eaten my mother's cooking.

Everyone laughs. JOHN and BEN finish their wine. MARIA gets up to get the coffee.
ELEANOR gets up to assist.

                             JOHN
This is a tasty port, Straw. Where'd you chance upon it?

                              BEN
Bought it over in Junction City. A grocer over there imports a nice stock of wines and
liquors. I think a good wine makes a meal more...digestible.

                             JOHN
                          (laughing)
And the company prettier?

                              BEN
                    (leaning back, smiling)
Oh, I wouldn't have Maria change one bit. She's everything I need in a woman...very
carnosa.
                    (he signs "large breasts")
Your being a newlywed, I'd think Eleanor would be enough woman for you.

                             JOHN
Indeed.

The women return with a chocolate cake and coffee. ELEANOR pours the coffee, while MARIA,
occasionally licking the frosting with enjoyment, cuts and serves the cake.

BEN
I hear you have an audience with the queen tomorrow.

                                    JOHN
The queen?

                                  ELEANOR
Is she really as...bad as Maria says?

                                    JOHN
She who? Bad how?

                                   MARIA
You'll see I'm not exaggerating.

                                     BEN
Your wife has been summoned by the Lieutenant Colonel's wife for an inspection.

                                    JOHN
Custer's wife?

                                     BEN
Elizabeth I'll-bring-home-the-Bacon-myself Custer.

                                   MARIA
Ben, querido. You really shouldn't talk about her that way.

                                     BEN
Why not? She thinks she's more of a man than her husband, although she'd never admit
she thinks that. But the way she pushes and promotes him herself, just so she seems to
be somebody, you'd think...

                                   MARIA
Ben, please.

                                     BEN
Alright. Just don't say I didn't warn you, Eleanor. Better spit shine your shoes and
polish your buttons, is all I've got to say.

INT PAYNE BEDROOM MORNING
The bed is made and ELEANOR is almost finished dressing. JOHN is gone. ELEANOR hears a
knock on the door.

                                 MARIA (OS)
You hoo! It's me. Are you ready?

ELEANOR grabs a cloth handbag by its string ties, takes one last look at herself and starts
downstairs.

                                  ELEANOR
I'm coming, Maria.

EXT FRONT PORCH OF TOWNHOUSE SAME MORNING
ELEANOR comes out the door, quietly closing the screen door behind her. MARIA is standing at the rail surrounding the porch, watching soldiers drilling on the nearby parade grounds. A group of Indians, several women, one old man and several children walk by. The women are dressed in cheery calicos and carry woven bags of foodstuffs. The little girls are dressed like their mothers. The old man and the boys wear calico shirts and jeans. ELEANOR and MARIA watch them go by.

                              ELEANOR
        Pretty babies.

                              MARIA
        Pretty women. Are you nervous?

                              ELEANOR
        Should I be?

                              MARIA
        I was. But then I'd heard about her before from other officer wives at other posts.

                              ELEANOR
        She's that talked about?

MARIA smiles wisely, looking sideways at ELEANOR.

                              MARIA
        Ambitious women are always subjects for discussion. Especially by other women.

EXT FORT RILEY STREET SAME MORNING
A cavalry company with Indian scouts ride by as ELEANOR and MARIA walk along the narrow dirt road to where it joins a broader street. Here, there are stately brick houses set back on plush, well-tended lawns. Piano music drifts down from the Custer house.

                              ELEANOR
                            (impressed)
Are you sure we're still in Kansas?

                              MARIA
        That's their house down there. The second one from the end.

                              ELEANOR
        Who lives in the one on the end?

                              MARIA
        That's the commander's house. The colonel and his wife live there.

                              ELEANOR
        Colonel Brown's? Why hasn't his wife asked to see me?

                              MARIA
        Officers wives are ranked just like their husbands. It's the second in command's duty to see to trivial details like seeing to new officers, so it's the second wife in command's duty to test new officers' wives.

ELEANOR

Test the wives? What kind of testing?

MARIA
(shrugs)
I don't know the wheres and the whyfors. I'm sure this system has been around as long as soldiers' wives have been. But, well, it's to make sure you understand the pecking order around here and aren't the kind of woman who'd try to step out of line.

ELEANOR

Pecking order? I'm not sure I enjoy being likened to a chicken.

MARIA
(laughs)
What do you mean? Men have been categorizing the kind of bird you are since you were born, amiga. Where have you been?

ELEANOR

Living like a man, I guess.

MARIA looks at ELEANOR sideways to see how to take the joke, then laughs. ELEANOR takes a deep breath, lifts one edge of her skirt and starts up the walk to the Custer house. MARIA follows one step behind.

INT CUSTER PARLOR SAME MORNING
A white MAID shows ELEANOR and MARIA into the room. ELIZABETH (LIBBIE) CUSTER, a small woman with a tiny waist, but a self-assured air about her, sits at the piano playing and singing "Carry Me Back to Ole Virginny". Three other women are already seated on the horsehair sofa and two are in horsehair chairs (other than MARIA, none come from an obvious ethnic background other than Old World European). While one woman softly sings along, the rest pretend rapt attention. ELEANOR and MARIA are shown to leather covered Victorian chairs as LIBBY continues to play. One of the women on the couch leans toward the one in the middle and whispers in her ear. The middle woman passes the message on to the woman on the other end of the couch (who is the one singing), who leans forward and nods in agreement toward the woman on the opposite end. MARIA and ELEANOR exchange looks, then MARIA leans in toward ELEANOR, who is removing her gloves.

MARIA
(whispers)
The women on the couch are all majors' wives. They're next in importance behind Mrs. Custer. The other two women are lieutenants.

LIBBY CUSTER finishes playing with flair. The women on the couch are quick to gently applaud; the others follow suit. LIBBY rises and bows with a grandiose sweep of her hands.

1ST MAJOR WIFE
Brava, brava, Libby. Your playing is wonderful, as always.

2ND MAJOR WIFE
Yes, Libby. That piece was divine. Did Autie bring that back from Washington on his last trip?

LIBBY picks up a fan and fans herself before sitting in a high-backed leather chair.

LIBBY

Oh, dear, no. Autie's always too busy when he's on Army business to browse through music shops.

1ST LIEUTENANT WIFE
(excitedly)

Oh, but I heard he saw Maggie Mitchell in *Little Barefoot* at the Palace Theater. A front row seat, even.

Because they aren't sure how LIBBY handles the rumors of her husband's infidelity, two of the majors' wives look at each other significantly, while the third glares at the thoughtless lieutenant's wife. MARIA senses it's time to change the subject and stands.

MARIA

Libby, I'd like you to meet Captain Payne's bride, Eleanor.

LIBBY stands and crosses over to ELEANOR before ELEANOR can stand. They are nearly eye to eye anyway. LIBBY takes ELEANOR's gloved hand and looks her right in the eye for a moment before she speaks.

LIBBY

Eleanor, I'm delighted to meet you. You're from Boston, I hear. I've never been there, so you must tell me all about it sometime.
(looks at ELEANOR's hands)
My, what long fingers you have, dear. Do you play the piano, too?

ELEANOR looks at LIBBY and is disconcerted by her direct eye contact. She turns and looks at MARIA, who smiles encouragingly. She turns and looks around the room at the other women, who wait expectantly.

ELEANOR
(retrieving her hand as gently as possible)

No, I'm afraid I don't, Mrs. Custer.

LIBBY

Please, call me Libby. And I hope I may call you Eleanor.

LIBBY smiles a practiced smile and turns to the other women as though taking another bow. She steps over to a table and rings a bell. A tall, thin black woman, ELIZA, appears with a tray heaped with hors d'oeurves, which she hands to LIBBY.

LIBBY

Thank you, Eliza. They look splendid. Did you save some for the General?

ELIZA

Yes, ma'am. I saved him a dozen, as you told me to. Should I save him some of the punch, too?

LIBBY

No, I don't think he'd find it stout enough. You can serve it any time.

ELIZA prepares to leave after giving LIBBY a short nod, taking the time to look at the women gathered in the room. She stares at ELEANOR the longest. ELEANOR smiles uncomfortably, touching her chin to feel for possible stubble.

LIBBY (CONT)
Help yourselves, ladies; we don't stand on ceremony around here.

LIBBY picks passes the tray around, with each woman taking just one hors d'oeuvre dantily.

1ST MAJOR WIFE
These are delicious, Libby. Eliza is certainly a blessing, isn't she?

2ND MAJOR WIFE
Indeed. Where did she learn to make them so...moist?

ELEANOR is having problems eating hers. She leans toward MARIA and whispers, as the other women continue to chatter. She's surprised MARIA has already eaten hers.

ELEANOR
How can you eat this? It tastes like...like...I don't know what. What is it?

MARIA
A sort of pate, I guess. I thought it was...all right. What's wrong with yours?

ELEANOR shrugs and stuffs the hors d'oeuvre in her mouth, swallowing with some difficulty. ELIZA returns with the punch and ELEANOR eagerly drinks hers. The other women look on in mild amazement.

LIBBY
Do you hunt, Eleanor?

ELEANOR
(clears her throat)
Hunt?

LIBBY
Yes, fox hunt. Ride with the hounds?

ELEANOR
Yes, once or twice, in England, actually. But...

LIBBY
But what, dear?

ELEANOR
There's fox hunting here?

LIBBY
Yes, the General takes us out with his hounds, Rover, Butcher, Otto and the others, to break the monotony on occasion. Would you care to join us sometime?

ELEANOR
Well, yes, except...

LIBBY
Except?

ELEANOR

I've never hunted sidesaddle before, and I'm afraid my husband won't let me ride any other way now.

LIBBY laughs and the other women follow suit.

LIBBY

I'm surprised that the English, who seem so refined, would allow a woman to hunt astride. I'm afraid I'll have to side with your husband, Eleanor. But don't worry, it's safe enough here on the prairie.

ELEANOR smiles tentatively and looks at MARIA, who sips her punch instead.

ELEANOR

Mrs. Custer, I mean Libby, I don't want to appear ignorant, but I'm afraid I'm rather new at all of this. Who is the General?

LIBBY

Why, General Custer, of course.

The women all laugh again.

INT THE PAYNE BEDROOM EVENING
JOHN is laughing heartily as he lies, at ease, on the bed, boots off, with his upper body leaning against the headboard, propped up by pillows. ELEANOR is pacing the room, occasionally stopping to lean on one of the posts at the foot of the bed.

ELEANOR

Go ahead, laugh. You never told me it'd be like this.

JOHN

What was to tell?

ELEANOR

Tea parties? Pecking orders, servants, fox hunting, predatory women, awful hors d'oeuvres. No. You let me worry about Indians, a peaceable people who are hundreds of miles away, but you didn't tell me about the real dangers.

JOHN

You're the one who had the dime novel ideas about the West, remember? I learned a long time ago that telling people back East what life was really like here would either lead them to think me a liar or entice them out here. And, as far as I'm concerned, it's too crowded here already.

ELEANOR

Crowded is right. I've never felt so confined before. But fox hunting? In a spine breaking sidesaddle?

JOHN

Believe me, I've been on several of these little excursions with Custer. The hounds always outpace us and we, officers and gentlemen that we are, hang back and ride with the ladies. It's more of a social event, not a real hunt.

                                        ELEANOR
Do I have to address Custer as General or as Lt. Colonel?

                                         JOHN
Only Custer, Libby, and his servants call him General. He might still consider himself a
Civil War general, but he's only drawing Lt. Colonel pay.

                                        ELEANOR
                                    (sits beside JOHN)
This is all a little overwhelming. I thought we'd be more...alone. That I'd keep house,
bake cakes and roast chickens, and you'd do whatever it is you do, come home, eat the
meals I so lovingly produced, then spend the rest of the time with me.

                                         JOHN
We're alone now.

ELEANOR smiles knowingly. JOHN smiles back. They kiss.

EXT   PARADE GROUNDS   EARLY MORNING
ELEANOR and JOHN, dressed for fox hunting, she in the only suit she brought, he in a more
casual, but still military uniform, sit astride their horses. Two of the majors' wives and one
lieutenant's wife, and their husbands, are also mounted and waiting. Several single officers,
many who imitate CUSTER's typical attire with buckskin pants and large Bolero hat, and one
INDIAN SCOUT fill out the hunting party. Dogs are barking in the background. Everyone
turns to look where the sound comes from. LIBBY, smartly decked out, sits astride her mount
as it ambles toward the group. A BLACK MAN holds onto the leashes of several staghounds
and beagles as they drag him across the grounds behind LIBBY.

                                         JOHN
                                    (to ELEANOR)
Ben is officer of the day, so he won't be here. Maria doesn't hunt?

                                        ELEANOR
No, she's afraid she'd break a horse's back jumping over a fence.

                                         JOHN
There are very few fences out here.

LIBBY reins her horse to a halt. The other horses stir because of the proximity of the barking
dogs.

                                         LIBBY
The General asked me to send his apologies. He was suddenly called away to Washington
yesterday, but wanted us to go ahead and enjoy ourselves, gladly giving us loan of his dogs.

                                      FIRST MAJOR
                                       (Swedish)
That was very generous of him, Mrs. Custer. But, if you'd rather not go without him, I'm
sure we'll all understand.

                              LIBBY
Oh, no! I insist and fully plan to participate with vigor, myself. Besides, a couple of the
professors from the university over in Manhattan plan to meet us near the Konza River.
I wouldn't want to disappoint them. Shall we go?

The MAN releases the dogs, who start off eagerly toward the eastern edge of the fort's land. The
party of riders follows along at a walk, then a trot, chatting amiably.

EXT   PRAIRIE   MORNING
The hounds are chasing a coyote which lopes over rise after rise almost as if leading the dogs on
deliberately. After the hounds pass, still following the coyote, the riders come into view, LIBBY
and several of the single officers lead the way. JOHN is ahead, then drops back to check on
ELEANOR, who is trying to bear the sidesaddle gracefully.

                              JOHN
                    (loping his horse beside ELEANOR's)
       How are you?

                            ELEANOR
                  (through gritted teeth, but smiling forcibly)
       Lovely. Just lovely.

From the right, a group of riders, three men and a woman, also outfitted for hunting, race
toward the hunting party.

                              JOHN
       Must be the university people.

LIBBY and several others stop their horses, while the rest race on after the hounds. ELEANOR
waves JOHN on and pulls up beside the stopped group. No one takes particular notice of her,
except NEISMAN, now a professor at the university.

                              LIBBY
       ...couldn't come, but we're so delighted you found us.

                         FIRST MALE RIDER
       Well, you're a bit off from where we said we'd meet, but we heard the hounds and knew
       where to find you.

                              LIBBY
       Excellent. Shall we continue the pursuit, then?

Most of the group follows LIBBY onward. ELEANOR groans and rubs her back and watches
them go on. One of the new riders, PROF. NEISMAN, comes up to her, pulling up alongside
her horse.

                            NEISMAN
       Are you all right, ma'am?

                            ELEANOR
                            (startled)
       Yes, I...it's just my back. I'm not used to riding sidesaddle so much.

ELEANOR recognizes the slightly older NEISMAN, but she isn't panicked that he might recognize her. She's amused, in fact, that he doesn't.

                              NEISMAN
        Perhaps if I...rub it for you?

NEISMAN sidles up closer and reaches over to rub ELEANOR's back. ELEANOR watches his face carefully for a sign of recognition.

                              ELEANOR
        Why, professor, do you give back rubs like this to all the women in sidesaddle?

                              NEISMAN
                        (smiling lecherously)
        Only when they need it.
                        (gives one last rub)
        I think we'd better catch up to the rest of the group, Miss....

                              ELEANOR
        Mrs.... Mrs. John Payne. And you are?

                              NEISMAN
        Prof. Edward Neisman, at your service, Mrs. Payne.

                              ELEANOR
                        (coquetishly)
        I'll have to remember that, Prof. Neisman.

ELEANOR kicks her horse into a lope. NEISMAN follows suit, catching up with her quickly. ELEANOR, with a mischievious grin on her face, kicks her horse harder. NEISMAN gives chase.

INT   PAYNE KITCHEN   EARLY EVENING
Maria is fixing dinner, occasionally adding a stick of wood to the stove as she works. ELEANOR peels potatoes. MARIA keeps glancing at ELEANOR, who is deep in reverie.

                              MARIA
        You know, ever since you returned from the hunt, you've been positively stoney. Yet there's this little glow about you, too. You're not pregnant, are you?

                              ELEANOR
        Pregnant, me? Oh dear, no.

                              MARIA
        How can you be so sure? Are you having your monthly flow?

                              ELEANOR
                        (hoping to silence MARIA)
        Maria, really. Such talk in the kitchen?

                              MARIA
        Where else would be more appropriate? You know, you shouldn't be handling food if you are...you know.

ELEANOR

No, I don't know. What on earth are you talking about?

MARIA

They must raise girls differently in Boston, is all I've got to say. You mean your mother didn't warn you you could die if you touched water when your period was on? Or that you'll contaminate food
                    (takes away the potatoes)
with your menstral odors?

ELEANOR

Don't be ridiculous.
                    (takes potatoes back)
Now let me finish this in peace, will you? I swear, you're worse than a mother hen.

MARIA

See, even you're talking chickens now.

EXT   PAYNE/STRAW BACKYARD   MORNING

Bright sunshine, blue skies and a light breeze reveal ELEANOR shooing several chickens away from her wash line, then finishing hanging up her wash, which dances gently in the early autumn air. As she pours out the remainder of her wash water, MARIA comes out with a basket load of clothes.

MARIA

Up with the chickens this morning, I see.

ELEANOR

Speaking of chickens, isn't there any way to keep these penned up so they don't do their business all over the yard?

MARIA

Pen up a chicken? That would ruin the quality of the eggs.
                    (pours water into tub)
You do like fresh eggs, don't you?

ELEANOR

Yes, but these are your chickens. Isn't there some way you can keep them on your side of the yard?

MARIA
(offended)

Haven't I shared the eggs, not to mention heaps of other food, with you?

ELEANOR

Well, yes, but...

MARIA
(near tears)

Are you saying you want to end our friendship just because of some chickens?

                         ELEANOR
                        (defensive)
No, that's not what I meant at all.

                          MARIA
                       (suspicious)
Are you going to see Libby today?

                         ELEANOR
Well, yes, aren't you? Weren't you invited to tea this afternoon?

MARIA busies herself with hanging her laundry, trying to recover her dignity.

                          MARIA
No, I wasn't.

                         ELEANOR
I'm sorry.

                          MARIA
Don't be. It's not your fault.

                         ELEANOR
I didn't know her friendship meant so much to you.

                          MARIA
Libby isn't anyone's friend, but it doesn't reflect well on...Ben, if she doesn't invite me.

                         ELEANOR
I had no idea she had such influence.

                          MARIA
Any woman worth her salt influences her husband's decisions.

                         ELEANOR
                        (laughing)
Surely, you're not as serious as you sound. A man will make his own decisions
regardless of what his wife thinks. Especially when it comes to business.

                          MARIA
                        (smiling)
You're still a newlywed yet.

                         ELEANOR
So?

                          MARIA
Eleanor. Unless he's a brute, a man won't force himself on you if you say no. The longer
you say no, the more influence you wield.

                         ELEANOR
                        (amused)
Maria. I had no idea you were such a conniving woman.

MARIA

Aren't you?

ELEANOR shakes her head, semi-seriously. She picks up her empty basket and waves back to MARIA as she enters the house.

INT   CUSTER PARLOR   AFTERNOON
LIBBY sits in her highbacked chair. She's in an elaborate white dress with a matching spray of baby's breath in her pinned up hair. Two of the majors' wives sit on the sofa. ELEANOR sits in a chair near the window, opposite LIBBY. All four women hold tea cups and saucers, with little crispy cookies lining the edges of their saucers. A tray of such goodies sits beside the tea pot on the center table. No one is saying anything. ELEANOR bites from a cookie and has some trouble getting the crumbs off her face, but she manages. The other women sip their tea occasionally.

ELEANOR

These biscuits are quite tasty, Libby.

LIBBY
(as though in reverie)

Biscuits?

FIRST MAJOR WIFE

I believe she means the cookies, dear.

LIBBY

Oh yes, the cookies. Thank you, Eleanor. Eliza made them especially for today.

SECOND MAJOR WIFE

I must get the recipe for them.

LIBBY

I'm sure Eliza would be flattered.

The ensuing silence hangs heavy. ELEANOR shifts uncomfortably.

ELEANOR
(clearing her throat)
I don't mean to pry, Libby, but...

Everyone turns to look at ELEANOR suspiciously.

ELEANOR (CONT)
I'm sorry. I don't know what else to do.

LIBBY
(almost impatiently)

What is it, Eleanor?

ELEANOR

I've noticed that you seem...

Everyone stares even more intently.

ELEANOR (CONT)
...rather preoccupied. Is there something wrong?

LIBBY lets out a big sigh and puts the back of her hand to her mouth rather melodramatically.
The majors' wives look put out with ELEANOR. ELIZA comes to the doorway. She takes time
to survey the room and its occupants before speaking.

ELIZA
Mrs. Custer, there's a gentleman caller here. He says he's from the university. Rode in
the hunt with you the other day. He's come to pay his respects.

LIBBY
Show him in, Eliza. And bring us a fresh pot of tea.

ELIZA nods, looks ELEANOR in the eye, and retreats. LIBBY tries to perk herself up by going
to the piano.

LIBBY
Let's show the professor how gay we can be, shall we?

LIBBY begins playing and singing "In the Gloaming" by Annie Fortescue Harrison. ELISA
returns with Prof. NEISMAN, who is dressed as he was for the hunt, carrying his hat in his
hand. He nods to the majors' wives first, then to ELEANOR. He pauses while making eye
contact with her to smile lasciviously at her. She notices the majors' wives noticing and shifts
uncomfortably but offers her only gloved hand (carefully holding her teacup in the other) to the
professor, who kisses it a little too long. LIBBY stops in the middle of the song, noticing, too.
Everyone looks at LIBBY. The professor gallantly bows toward the piano.

NEISMAN
Ah, Mrs. Custer. You look so radiant today. Almost as if you were fresh from the hunt.

LIBBY
You're looking rather fresh yourself, Prof. Neisman. Ladies, you've all had the pleasure
of making Prof. Neisman's aquaintance, I assume.

LIBBY looks significantly at ELEANOR. ELEANOR straightens her spine and looks her back in
the eye. She speaks in a lustily deep voice.

ELEANOR
Yes, Libby. I've had that honor.

Prof. NEISMAN smiles, sensing a minor squabble over him. He sits in a chair close to
ELEANOR.

NEISMAN
I understand the General was called to Washington rather suddenly, Mrs. Custer. I'll never
understand how any man could ever leave your side for more than a few minutes.

LIBBY beams triumphantly, moving from the piano to NEISMAN's side. Taking his hand, she
pulls him to his feet.

LIBBY
You flatter me, Professor. Have I ever shown you my husband's prized collection of
books?

LIBBY begins to lead him out of the parlor, then remembers her other guests.

                    LIBBY (CONT)
Eleanor, I don't believe I've had the chance to show you either. Will you two ladies
entertain yourselves, while the three of us dash upstairs to peek at the library.

The majors' wives are a bit put out but continue to sit on the sofa. ELEANOR sets her cup and
saucer down and follows LIBBY and NEISMAN out.

INT UPSTAIRS HALLWAY OF CUSTER HOUSE
LIBBY is still leading the professor by the hand. He looks back at ELEANOR and shrugs once
while LIBBY chatters.

                    LIBBY
Being a man of letters, I'm sure you'll find the collection miniscule, but immaculate.
Autie would be honored to know you took the time to examine it, though, Prof.
Neisman.

                    NEISMAN
The honor's all mine, I'm sure.

INT CUSTER LIBRARY
LIBBY leads them into a small corner room. On each of two sides, large two pane windows look
out onto trees whose leaves are falling. Opposite the windows, two walls have large bookcases
built into the walls. The cases are filled, but not full, with various adornments, like figure busts,
filling in gaps. A fairly large wooden desk and leather chair sit catty-corner so that the chair's
occupant can see out either window. Several papers are neatly stacked to one side. An
elaborate pen holder sits at the top of the desk. A small red book sits in the center of the large
paper blotter covering the desktop.

NEISMAN approaches the bookcases and begins reading spines. LIBBY watches him, hoping
for a sign of pleasure. ELEANOR moves silently toward the windows and peers out. As she
watches LIBBY dote on NEISMAN, she crosses to the desk and picks up the book on the blotter.
Its spine says JOURNAL in gold lettering. She looks up to see if LIBBY or NEISMAN notices,
then opens the cover of the book. The inside leaf says, in a floral script, "The personal diary of
Elizabeth Bacon Custer." ELEANOR is startled when NEISMAN clears his throat.

                    NEISMAN
              (looking in ELEANOR's direction)
As I was saying, Mrs. Custer...

                    LIBBY
Oh, please, professor, call me Libby.

                    NEISMAN
It would be an honor...Libby.
              (looks toward ELEANOR)
As I was saying, Libby, this is a fine collection of books. Did you help the General put it
together?

                    LIBBY
Well, I...I don't want to seem immodest, but...yes, I chose several of these for him.
Bought several for him, myself....professor.

NEISMAN

I must commend you on your impeccable taste, Libby. Please, call me Edward.

LIBBY

Thank you....

(with emphasis)

Edward.

NEISMAN
(turning to face ELEANOR)

And you, too, Mrs. Payne. I would consider it an honor if you would be so kind as to consider me enough of a...friend to call me, Edward, as well.

LIBBY steps back, watching ELEANOR and NEISMAN's friendly, familiar interaction.

INT   PAYNE BEDROOM   NIGHT

Through the window, a half moon shines across beds of fallen leaves and half-nude trees. The moonlight stretches across the floor and over the bed, where JOHN and ELEANOR are making love. JOHN is amorous, ELEANOR less receptive. Finally, JOHN lies back and sits up against the headboard.

JOHN

You're not in the mood tonight.

ELEANOR

Sorry.

JOHN
(turning the bedside lamp up)

You seem really preoccupied. Is something bothering you?

ELEANOR

No...no...I'm just...tired.

JOHN

Living in the wild west is getting to you?

ELEANOR

Wild West. It can't be too wild if there are universities with professors out here.

JOHN

You still thinking about your encounter with Neisman at the hunt?

ELEANOR

I encountered him again today.

JOHN

Oh? Been sneaking off to Manhattan behind my back? Was it as good as you remembered?

ELEANOR
(grimacing)

Don't be cruel. I saw him at the Custers'.

                              JOHN
Oh, yeah. Ben mentioned Maria got the brush-off today. I told him not to worry. The real man of the house has gone to Washington.

                            ELEANOR
                      (rolling her eyes at him)
You're as bad as the rest. Libby, despite her need for adulation, isn't a bad person. I think she's really very lonely, especially since her husband seems to prance around on her frequently.

                              JOHN
                            (mocking)
Prance around on her?

                            ELEANOR
You know what I mean. He's got some woman back in Washington.

                              JOHN
Yeah, she's called the U.S. Army.

                            ELEANOR
No, I'm serious. She's an actress or something.

                              JOHN
I know. I've heard the rumors. I just think you're taking Mrs. Custer's problems too seriously.

JOHN gets up and goes to the dresser, picking up a cigar. He bites off the end and lights it.

                            ELEANOR
And what if I fooled around on you? How would that make you feel?

                              JOHN
You fool around on me and you're liable to get us both hanged for illegal fornication with
                      (mock ominously)
the same sex.

                            ELEANOR
Don't tell me that on those long tours of duty out on the plains when you troopers have to share beds to stay warm that there's no shenanigans going on. I know better.

JOHN moves over to the chair by the window, picks up and slips on his pants.

                              JOHN
I'm hungry. How 'bout you?

                            ELEANOR
                          (exasperated)
John! Aren't you going to answer me?

                              JOHN
I didn't know you asked a question.

JOHN disappears through the doorway.

                              ELEANOR
                             (shouting)
        Aren't you going to tell me?

                               JOHN
                          (shouting back)
        Shh! The walls have ears.

MONTAGE:
INT   JUNCTION CITY DRY GOODS STORE   DAY
ELEANOR and MARIA are shopping. A couple of women (who will reappear later), wives of
enlisted men, with several children in tow pay for their goods and leave. MARIA is looking at
cloth; ELEANOR looks at books. She finds a JOURNAL like LIBBY's and picks it up, opening
the book so that the spine makes a cracking sound. She turns the pages, all empty, and smiles.
Closing the book, she puts it on the counter with her other purchases. The clerk puts it in a box
with everything else.

INT PAYNE KITCHEN EARLY AFTERNOON
ELEANOR unpacks the groceries and dry goods from Junction City. She lingers over the
Journal, rubbing its spine with her hand.

INT FIRST FLOOR HALLWAY
Carrying the Journal and humming "Hiding in Thee," ELEANOR begins to climb the stairs.

INT PAYNE LIBRARY
She carries the Journal into the little library she has set up in a back room upstairs. A small
desk with a chair sits in front of the one window facing out into the backyard where chickens
are scattered. One bookcase is against the opposite wall, with about 10 books tidily lined on a
shelf. She sets the Journal on the desk blotter.

INT PAYNE PARLOR MID AFTERNOON
ELEANOR is cleaning. She dusts all the knickknacks, wipes down the shelves and wooden
furniture, cleans the inside of the windows. She stops to look out, watching a small group of
soldiers drill on the parade grounds across the street. She rests a hand on the glass, watching it
steam up the glass and smiles.

INT PAYNE KITCHEN LATE AFTERNOON
ELEANOR finishes peeling potatoes and puts a large pot of them on to boil. Drying her hands,
she takes off her apron and sets it on the table.

INT   PAYNE LIBRARY   AFTERNOON
ELEANOR enters, turning up a lamp to the growing gloom. She looks at a small mantle clock
she has on the top of the bookcase. It's 4:45. After carefully opening a new bottle of ink, she
opens the journal to the first cover leaf and picks up a quill pen. Very carefully, she writes:
"The personal diary of Eleanor Payne." She blows the words dry, then presses back the page
and dates the next one: "October 15, 1874." She takes a deep breath and begins to write:
"What a life I'm leading." As she writes, we move back to the window.

EXT   PAYNE BACKYARD
In the backyard, through the window, we see the final leaves fall from the tree, snow fall, melt,
and buds come out.

INT   PAYNE LIBRARY   AFTERNOON
Pulling back inside, ELEANOR, whose dress and general appearance has changed to reflect the passage of time, is finishing an entry for May 15, 1875: "Prof. Neisman is coming to tea." As she finishes writing the line, MARIA calls up to her from downstairs.

MARIA (OS)
Eleanor, the professor just pulled up in his buggy. Should I set out the canapes?

ELEANOR
Yes. And please put the kettle on for tea?

ELEANOR closes the journal, stands and runs her hands down her skirt, briefly touches her hair, then leans down to peer out the back window where chickens are scattered. She hears a bell ring at the front door and listens for MARIA to answer it. She steps out of the room to the head of the stairs and peers down.

INT   PAYNE PARLOR   AFTERNOON
MARIA shows NEISMAN a comfortable chair, one of a pair next to a small table. She excitedly excuses herself just as ELEANOR steps into the room. NEISMAN stands again, gallantly taking ELEANOR's hand and kissing the back of it after making sure MARIA is gone.

NEISMAN
Eleanor, you look radiant.
(looking in direction MARIA exited)
I didn't know we'd...have company today. I was in hopes it would just be the two of us.

ELEANOR
(offering a canape from tray on table)
Edward! How forward of you. You know how tongues would wag if you visited me now unchaperoned, what with John away on a campaign and me all alone here.

NEISMAN smiles and bites off a bit of the canape as though he's being sexually suggestive. ELEANOR demurely, coyly, sits in one of the chairs, setting the tray on the table. NEISMAN starts to sit in the opposite chair, but motions toward the sofa.

NEISMAN
Don't you think we'd be more comfortable over here?

ELEANOR
Comfort is something I'm not willing to give you, just yet, professor.

NEISMAN sits in the chair opposite ELEANOR with an almost childlike grin of glee on his face.

NEISMAN
You mean that there's hope that you will? Soon?

MARIA enters with a pot of tea and three cups on another tray. She's overheard part of the conversation and doesn't approve, exhibiting her displeasure in a scowl. She sets the tray down on another small table in front of the sofa with much ado and noise.

MARIA
I assume we're all ready for tea now.

ELEANOR

Yes, Maria, we're ready.

MARIA begins pouring tea and handing out cups. As she hands NEISMAN his, she begins interrogating him.

MARIA

So, professor, how is this term going? Any problems among your students? Anyone caught cheating
(looks at ELEANOR)
recently?

NEISMAN

No. I'm happy to report, Mrs. Straw, that my students have been perfect angels this term.

MARIA

Is that unusual, professor?

NEISMAN
(looking at ELEANOR)
No, indeed, Mrs. Straw. I've always been known as a teacher who puts his students through their paces. They don't dare get out of line with me as their master.

ELEANOR

You make it sound as if your students are all animals, professor.

NEISMAN

Young men at this age can be, I assure you, Mrs. Payne. You're fortunate to be dealing with me, instead of them. They have absolutely no control over their baser needs.

MARIA
(between sips)
So you set an example for them, do you?

EXT   FLINT HILLS   AFTERNOON
ELEANOR and NEISMAN ride in his buggy on a well-worn strip of dirt road. The afternoon is sunny and warm. Birds sing and fly up as the horse and buggy pass. The rolling hills are fecund with tall green, swaying grasses and flowers. NEISMAN steers the horse off the road and up a knoll, pulling to a halt at the end of the ridge. The hills roll away like lounging bodies before them. The fort is visible three or four miles away. They get out of the buggy and walk a little ways away.

NEISMAN

And all this could be yours, Eleanor.

ELEANOR

You're so generous. How magnanimous of you to give me something you don't even own.

NEISMAN

Farmers give up their homesteads all the time. It wouldn't be much of a trick to buy a decent plot of land to raise a few chickens on.

ELEANOR
You expect to quit the university and try your hand at raising chickens?

NEISMAN
(laughs)
Oh, the chickens aren't for me. They're for you.

ELEANOR
And what would I want with a bunch of chickens?

NEISMAN
You could collect the eggs and sell them for some income of your own, while I do the important things like teach.

ELEANOR
Oh. I see. This is your way of telling me to leave my husband and come live with you? How does the verse go? "Come live with me and be my love and we will all the pleasures prove"?

NEISMAN
(putting his arm around her)
Exactly.

ELEANOR
Why, Professor Neisman, I could never leave my husband.

NEISMAN
What's he got that I haven't got?
(kisses her)

ELEANOR
I don't know. Maybe you could show me.

Entwined, and kissing passionately, they sink to the ground. NEISMAN eagerly pulls up ELEANOR's skirts and gropes upwards. He stops when he discovers something unexpected. He pulls away from kissing and looks at ELEANOR's face, then pulls up the skirt for a better look. He sits down hard and looks at ELEANOR's face again.

NEISMAN
You're...you're a...

ELEANOR
What's the matter, professor, has it been that long?

NEISMAN
Has what been that long?

ELEANOR
You mean you don't recognize me?

ELEANOR is genuinely surprised. She sits hastily up, instinctively pulling down her skirts

ELEANOR (CONT)
I thought you knew. I thought you were just playing along.

NEISMAN

Playing along?

NEISMAN scrutinizes ELEANOR's face, jerking back her hair for a better look. Finally, he recognizes her, and stands, clearly agitated, continually rubbing his mouth with the back of his hand.

NEISMAN (CONT)
Oh, my god, I know you now. Wright. Claypool Wright from Boston.

ELEANOR
Yes, it's me. Surprised?

NEISMAN begins spitting as though with a bitter taste in his mouth. He takes out a handkerchief and wipes his hands as though trying to get something off of them, moving continually further away.

NEISMAN
Oh god. I purged that...that...from me. I...I...never wanted to do that again. And now...now you've led me on. You almost let me.... And now you...look at you. You've become a fucking woman! How could you sink this low?

ELEANOR
I don't understand. I thought you said you would always...love men.

NEISMAN
I thought you were a woman! I...I...you don't understand. I found God, and a man should never lie with another man as he does a woman. It's sinful.

ELEANOR
(laughing scornfully)
A sin? You were just about to fornicate with another man's wife. What about "covet not thy neighbor's wife"? Isn't that a sin?

NEISMAN
Not as bad.
(defensively)
I might have married you...eventually. Made an honest woman of you.

ELEANOR
Made an honest woman of me!? Noble and decent human being that you are you might have eventually married me just to clear your own sinful conscience.

NEISMAN
(full implications hit him)
My god, Clay. Does Capt. Payne know?

He must. You've entered into a legal marriage with another man? You've committed, and probably continue to commit, sodomy under religious and government sanction?

ELEANOR has picked up her hat and is marching toward the buggy. NEISMAN runs after her.

NEISMAN
Oh, no you don't. Not in my buggy, you son of Sodom.

As ELEANOR tries to climb into the buggy, NEISMAN pushes her away, climbing into the buggy himself.

NEISMAN (CONT)
You can just walk back to the fort.

ELEANOR
Don't be ridiculous.

NEISMAN whips the horse into motion, leaving ELEANOR behind.

ELEANOR (CONT)
Wait! Edward! Wait!

NEISMAN stops, ELEANOR runs to catch up.

ELEANOR (CONT)
I knew you couldn't leave me.

NEISMAN
Oh no, you don't. I meant what I said. Just what do you think your husband's superiors would do to the two of you if they knew, huh? Probably string you up or at least tar and feather you. Maybe they'd even horsewhip you in front of the troops so no one else would get any ideas. Don't you think?

ELEANOR
No. You wouldn't. You can't.

NEISMAN
Oh? And just why not?

ELEANOR
What would your precious university do to you if they found out you were fired from Harvard for sleeping with a man you slept with again here? A man who dresses like a woman.

NEISMAN
I haven't slept with you here.

ELEANOR
And just who would they believe? A man who tried to seduce another man's wife and discovered she was male? The same man who was let go from Harvard for unsavory practices with his students?

NEISMAN
You were the only one. I swear.

ELEANOR
Do you think that would make much difference to them?

NEISMAN thinks over the threat. Grimaces and shrugs.

NEISMAN

You still walk back.

NEISMAN clucks the horse on. From our withdrawing bird's eye view: ELEANOR watches the buggy retreat, looks around at her isolation, then starts walking back to the fort.

When we pull back far enough, our gaze becomes that of a sentry on horseback on a nearby knoll who has apparently watched the scenario through a pair of binoculars. He laughs, then turns to his companion, passing off the binoculars.

FIRST SENTRY

Looks like the professor lucked out. She must not have been willing to give him any.

SECOND SENTRY

Think we should go rescue her? I'm sure Capt. Payne would be grateful.

FIRST SENTRY

Yeah, but then he'd want to know why she was abandoned out here. I'm not the messenger of infidelity for any man.

SECOND SENTRY

Think she'll be okay?

FIRST SENTRY

No Indians or bandits within miles.

SECOND SENTRY

Hate to see a woman treated that way.

FIRST SENTRY

From what I hear, she's more man than woman.

SECOND SENTRY

Oh?

The FIRST SENTRY smiles broadly and takes back his binoculars for one last look. Then he packs them in his saddlebag and turns his horse away. The SECOND SENTRY shades his eyes and tries to see ELEANOR. Disgusted either by his friend's cryptic words or with failing to find ELEANOR, he whips his horse to follow after his companion at a lope.

EXT   PAYNE PORCH   EARLY EVENING
A loveseat swing sits at the Payne end of the porch. Stationary chairs are at the Straw end. ELEANOR and MARIA rock side by side in wooden rockers in the middle. They are dressed nicely, in anticipation of their husbands' return from the field. For a brief period, they say nothing. MARIA, seemingly resolved to speak her mind, hestitantly speaks.

MARIA

I don't see what you see in him.

ELEANOR

Who?

                              MARIA
The professor. He's so old and he's not nearly as attractive as John.

                            ELEANOR
                      (not willing to discuss it)
You find John attractive?

                              MARIA
                           (defensive)
Don't change the subject. I just think...you owe John some...respect.

                            ELEANOR
I respect John.

                              MARIA
                    (turns defiantly to ELEANOR)
You come back from an afternoon outing with the...the lecherous professor, all hot and
sweaty, and this being one of the mildest springs I've known here, and you have the
audacity to tell me nothing happened?

                            ELEANOR
I didn't say that.

                              MARIA
So, you admit it! Something did happen.

                            ELEANOR
Yes.

                              MARIA
Oh my god! And you say you respect John, the man who risks his life daily to support
you?

                            ELEANOR
What happened is not what you think happened, Maria. You're so melodramatic.

                              MARIA
Perhaps you'd like to enlighten me, then?

Three riders appear just down the street. The men are singing "The Girl I Left Behind."
MARIA jumps up and runs to the steps. ELEANOR stands, stepping calmly up to the porch
railing.

                          MARIA (CONT)
They're coming.

                            ELEANOR
I see that.

The three riders, JOHN, BEN, and CAPTAIN ORA NASH (30ish, no distinctive ethnicity), ride
right up to the porch, still singing, and dismount. Nash holds the horses' reins, while the
husbands embrace their wives.

                                        BEN
Did you miss me?

                                       MARIA
Every second.

                                       JOHN
Did you miss me?

                                      ELEANOR
                                      (teasing)
Not one bit.

MARIA looks uncomfortably over at ELEANOR. Then down to NASH.

                                       MARIA
Who's your new friend?

                                        BEN
Ladies, this new lad is Captain Ora Nash. And don't let his good looks fool you. He's
one of the toughest men in a scrape I've ever known. Excepting me and John, here, of
course. Tie those horses up, Nash, and step on up. I'm sure, knowing my Maria, that
the women have planned a welcome home feast for us.

With a general air of merriment, the five disappear into the Straw side of the house.

MONTAGE:
INT STRAW DINING ROOM
The five people circle the dining table. JOHN has his arm around ELEANOR. MARIA sits as
close as possible to BEN, who is eating ravenously. ORA sits at the head of the table, singing .
ORA finishes the song, and everyone breaks into applause and laughter. Food is spread
banquet-like over the table.

INT PAYNE BEDROOM EARLY MORNING
ELEANOR is shaving her face at the wash basin. JOHN pretends to sneak up behind her,
wrestling the shaving blade from her hand, then kissing her passionately, getting the cream on
ELEANOR's face all over his own. They laugh when they look at each other.

INT OFFICERS' BALLROOM EVENING
The women are all elegantly dressed. The men are in dress uniform. ELEANOR and JOHN
waltz, clearly enjoying each other's company. BEN and MARIA dance, too, but not as
energetically. NASH, near the refreshment table, sips his punch and watches, focusing his
attention on ELEANOR and JOHN. They see him as they pass, and he raises his cup to them.

EXT PAYNE PORCH NIGHT
The five are sitting on the porch. NASH is strumming a guitar and singing. The others, coupled
off, listen dreamily. NASH continually looks toward ELEANOR and JOHN. Fireflies dance just
off the porch, and NASH's singing is overshadowed by the night sounds of insects and frogs.

EXT THE FLINT HILLS DAY
JOHN, ELEANOR (astride, not sidesaddle), and NASH are out for a ride. They ride up the
gentle rise of a hill and follow its crest to one end, which overlooks the rolling plains and a small
river. As they sit and admire it, NASH admires ELEANOR. JOHN notices with apparent
amusement and a touch of sadness.

INT   CUSTERS' PARLOR   AFTERNOON
Several of the officers' wives sit about chatting. Nash is seated next to ELEANOR. They are talking amiably with MARIA. LIBBY stands looking out the window. Through the double front windows, we see several officers smoking, one of whom, from the back, could be CUSTER (longish blond hair, blue military shirt and leather leggings). JOHN and BEN's faces can be seen. They are somber, listening intently to CUSTER.

INT   PAYNE BEDROOM   NIGHT
A lamp on the bedside table burns low. JOHN and ELEANOR are cuddled closely under the bed covers, talking in soft voices.

                              ELEANOR
     Is there any real danger?

                              JOHN
     Not here, no.

                              ELEANOR
     I mean for you.

                              JOHN
     Every campaign has its inherent dangers.

                              ELEANOR
     Everyone seems to be taking this campaign to round up the Sioux more seriously than
     they have others.

                              JOHN
     It just means more time in the field.

                              ELEANOR
     But aren't the Sioux talking war?

                              JOHN
     That's what we've been fighting already. They're just holding out a little longer before
     they'll give in and move onto the reservation. Believe me. Sitting Bull is a wise leader.
     He'll see this is the best way for his people.

                              ELEANOR
     Would you, if you were in his place?

JOHN doesn't reply. Instead, he looks away for a moment, then turns back and begins stroking ELEANOR's hair and face, eventually kissing her with more and more passion. ELEANOR responds in kind.

EXT   EDGE OF FORT GROUNDS   EARLY MORNING
It's early June. The sun is just rising. Mist covers the low-lying areas and long green grass carpets the earth. Three companies of cavalry soldiers are lined up, officers in the fore of each company, heading out of the fort. Wagonloads of supplies follow. In front, a good distance away, CUSTER and LIBBY, accompanied by three or four dogs, ride their horses. CUSTER and his horse seem unusually animated with CUSTER waving his arms and his horse prancing excitedly. The dogs yip and playfully bite at each other as they run about. Several Indian scouts (a mixture of Arikara, Crow, and Lakota) follow CUSTER, then the regular troops. Along the

road, officers' wives stand and wave with a good amount of dignity. Further along, enlisted men's wives stand, surrounded by children, waving and singing, "The Girl I Left Behind." Even further, toward the outskirts stand large groups of Indians (also composed of mixed Indian nations), solemnly watching the column snake its way toward the horizon.

ELEANOR, standing to one side holding her horse's reins, watches JOHN and his company march by, waving continually at them. Beside her stand NASH, BEN and MARIA. MARIA holds one hand across her stomach as though pregnant and has the other tucked under BEN's arm. The men salute the passing soldiers, especially JOHN.

>   BEN
> Wish I were going. I'd show those Indians a thing or two.

>   MARIA
> I'm glad you're not. Junior is glad, too.
>   (glancing at ELEANOR)
> I'm sure they'll all return safely though.

>   ELEANOR
> Libby can't stand to be without Autie, can she?

>   NASH
> Can you stand to be without John?

>   ELEANOR
> I hope I don't have to find out for long.

ELEANOR looks around to avoid seeing JOHN disappear over the rise, noticing that ELIZA is the only Custer servant to attend the send off. ELIZA appears expressionless as she exchanges glances with ELEANOR.

The enlisted men's wives and children stand along a scraggily fence that surrounds the married soldiers' barracks. The women, unlike the officers' wives, openly cry, some hold infants and toddlers up to see their fathers one last time. Several of the children mimic the soldiers by lining up and marching alongside the troops. One enterprising child has a piece of cloth tied to a stick and heads the child troops.

ELEANOR's attention turns back to the disappearing column of men and horses, searching for JOHN among them. Finally spotting him, she waves one last time, then turns away, leading her horse back toward the stables. NASH follows suit.

>   NASH
> Why didn't you ride out with John, the way Libby did with Custer?

>   ELEANOR
> I couldn't. I'm afraid I don't get wrapped up in all the pageantry and the hero worship, the way Libby does. Besides, I hate prolonged goodbyes. They hurt less if they're quick, like slicing the skin.

>   NASH
> Are you very much in love with John?

ELEANOR

What a strange question to ask a wife. If she answers yes, the man who asks is disappointed. If she answers no, the man who asks thinks less of the woman, even if he sees an opportunity for himself.

NASH

I didn't mean to offend you.

ELEANOR

Didn't you?

INT   CUSTER PARLOR   AFTERNOON
LIBBY is pointing to a map spread out on the center table. Several officers' wives listen attentively. Even ELEANOR leans close, despite the proximity of Prof. NEISMAN next to LIBBY.

LIBBY

According to Autie's last letter, they are here now, at the mouth of the Tongue River. He said he's not only had success in fishing from the river, but he shot an antelope on the march.

NEISMAN

Sounds as if they're having a wonderful time.

LIBBY

One thing that sobered Autie was a skull they found in an abandoned village. They found it next to the remnants of a cavalry uniform.

FIRST MAJOR WIFE

The savages.

ELEANOR
(stiffening)

Yes, we're so much more civilized. We not only alleviated the suffering of the warriors at Washita, we also ended it for the women and children. Then we end their horses' misery, as well. We're the epitome of the milk of human kindness all right.

NEISMAN

Don't you even care about your husband's life, Eleanor?

ELEANOR
(standing)

Of course. I've just never had a stomach for war.

EXT   PORCH OF PAYNE HOUSE   EARLY EVENING
A lamp, fastened to the outer wall, is lit. ELEANOR and MARIA are rocking. MARIA knits baby clothes. ELEANOR fans herself. Ben comes out to stand by the railing and lights a pipe.

BEN

Lovely evening, isn't it?

MARIA

Yes, it is.

MARIA stops rocking and puts a hand to her stomach. She smiles.

                          MARIA (CONT)
Ben Junior is impatient to come out and play. He just kicked me again.

                            ELEANOR
It must feel so good to feel life growing inside you. I wish I could have a child.

                             MARIA
                            (laughs)
It took Ben and I nearly eight years, Eleanor. Be patient, amiga. I'm sure you'll get your wish.

ELEANOR smiles sadly. Looking down the street toward the sound of an approaching horse.

                              BEN
It looks like Nash coming. You girls need to get together and fix him up with someone. He's a mighty lonely man.

MARIA giggles. NASH rides his horse up to the porch and dismounts.

                              BEN
Evening, Nash. What brings you out tonight?

                             NASH
                      (looking at ELEANOR)
I thought Mrs. Payne could use some company.

                             MARIA
                    (suspicious and scornful)
She's got Ben and I, doesn't she?

                             NASH
Do you mind my company, Mrs. Straw?

                             MARIA
                          (softening)
Not if you sing us a song.

                             NASH
I didn't bring my guitar.

                            ELEANOR
Try it *a capella* then.

                             NASH
Anything you'd like to hear?

                            ELEANOR
Anything but "The Girl I Left Behind" or "Nearer, My God, to Thee."

NASH settles on the loveseat-swing and begins to sing. Night sounds overtake his singing as we pull further and further away from the porch.

EXT   PAYNE PORCH   MORNING
It's Independence Day. The parade ground across from the house is decorated, and a portion of the military band plays patriotic songs. Women and children, and people from Manhattan and Junction City, sit in the stands watching the parade of soldiers--the few who are left at the fort. Children set off fireworks. ELEANOR and NASH sit next to each other in the rocking chairs on the porch.

                    ELEANOR
They should have encountered the Sioux by now, shouldn't they?

                    NASH
More than likely. We'll get news when the next steamer comes back down, probably in two days. Are you anxious?

                    ELEANOR
Libby said yesterday that she feels she's lost Autie already. She went on to say she didn't hold much stock in premonitions, though. Do you?

                    NASH
If a soldier worried about that, he'd never go into battle.

                    ELEANOR
                (attempting laughter)
If a woman acted on premonition, she'd never get married.

She looks at NASH, who smiles reassuringly back. He takes her hand and squeezes it. She squeezes back.

                ELEANOR (CONT)
I'll never forget how supportive you've been through this.

                    NASH
I understand what you're going through.

                    ELEANOR
You know, I wish you really did.

                    NASH
                (leaning forward)
Believe me when I say I do.

A burst of firecrackers startles them, and two boys run away laughing.

INT   PAYNE BEDROOM   EARLY MORNING
ELEANOR is sleeping fitfully. A volley of shots startles her awake, and she quickly gets out of bed, running to the window.

EXT   PAYNE HOUSE
BEN is leaning out the Straw bedroom window as ELEANOR peers out.

                    ELEANOR
What's going on?

                                BEN
        I don't know, but I'll find out.

BEN's head disappears inside. ELEANOR looks up and down the street, seeing men on
horseback at one end, with women running about in their nightgowns.

BEN, still pulling up his suspenders, dashes out the front door and down the porch steps.
MARIA sticks her head out the bedroom window.

                                MARIA
        Have you seen anything? Are we under attack?

                                ELEANOR
        I've only seen soldiers and women. No Indians. So I don't think we're under attack.

A woman screams in grief. Indian women's voices are raised in a sorrowful trill.

                                MARIA
        Oh my god.

                                ELEANOR
        They've heard. News has come back from the West. Bad news.

ELEANOR withdraws.

INT PAYNE BEDROOM
ELEANOR starts to dress, then realizes her face is stubbly.

                                ELEANOR
                            (to herself)
        Damn. This is no time to have to shave.

Quickly, she pours water and lathers up. She hears her front screen door slam shut and the
front door open and close. Footsteps, heavy and slow, sound on the stairs.

                                ELEANOR
        Maria, is that you?

                                MARIA (OS)
                         (huffing and puffing)
        Yes. Can I help you? Are you okay?

                                ELEANOR
        You shouldn't be climbing the stairs in your condition. Stay downstairs, I'll be down
        momentarily.

                                MARIA (OS)
        All right.

ELEANOR is finishing dressing after having shaved when she hears MARIA talking to someone
at the door.

                                SOLDIER (OS)
        Hello, Mrs. Straw, is Mrs. Payne here?

MARIA (OS)

Yes, she is. She's upstairs dressing. Shall I get her?

Other footsteps resound on the wooden steps.

MARIA (OS)

Ben? Ben, what's happened?

BEN (OS)

Where's Eleanor?

MARIA (OS)

Upstairs.

The sound of footsteps climbing the stairs makes ELEANOR sit down in defeat on the edge of the bed. BEN peers around the door jamb into the bedroom.

BEN

Eleanor?

ELEANOR

Yes, Ben.

BEN

Eleanor, John's been...

ELEANOR

Killed.

BEN

Yes. I'm so sorry. He went down fighting. He fought valiantly to the end. He and 200 other men.

ELEANOR

Two hundred?

BEN

It was a massacre.

ELEANOR begins to cry softly. BEN doesn't know what to do.

BEN (CONT)

Maria, come up here. I think Eleanor needs you.

INT   STAIRS
NASH helps MARIA carefully up the stairs.

INT   BEDROOM
Both enter the bedroom and sit on either side of ELEANOR. NASH looks up at BEN, who has remained by the door.

NASH

Go on. We'll take care of her.

ELEANOR leans on NASH and cries on his shoulder. He embraces her, rocking her gently. MARIA stands and crosses to BEN. She has almost reached him, when she grabs her stomach in pain.

                                         BEN
          Maria. Are you all right?

ELEANOR stops crying. She and NASH rush to help BEN ease MARIA to the floor.

                                       MARIA
          I think it's time.

                                         BEN
          Are you sure? It's too early.

MARIA cries out in pain again. Her water breaks and spills all over the floor. They all look at each other incredulously.

                                     ELEANOR
          Let's put her on the bed. Ora, go get a doctor. Ben, have whoever is still downstairs put
          some water on to boil, and you get some sheets out of that trunk over there.

The two men carry MARIA to the bed, then disappear out the door. ELEANOR begins soothing MARIA who is panicking.

                                       MARIA
          It's too early. By my calculations, I should have another month and a half yet.

                                     ELEANOR
          These things are never exact. Don't worry. My mother always told me I took twelve
          months to be born and twenty-five years to grow up. You're going to have a healthy,
          happy baby, amiga.

MARIA laughs, then cries out in pain.

INT   PAYNE BEDROOM   NIGHT
MARIA cries out in pain. She is covered in sweat. ELEANOR and LIBBY assist the doctor--
ELEANOR wipes MARIA's brow; LIBBY stands ready with fresh sheets--discarded bloody ones
are piled on the floor.

                                     DOCTOR
          You're doing just fine, Maria. I can see his head crowning now. You can push.

                                       LIBBY
          Push, dear. Push as hard as you can.

                                       MARIA
                                 (with much effort)
          I'm pushing. I'm pushing.

ELEANOR tries to watch what is happening between MARIA's legs, but can't stomach it for long. She concentrates on smiling at MARIA.

                          ELEANOR
You have names all picked out, don't you?

                          MARIA
Benjamin Junior, if it's a boy.
                              (pushes hard)
Eleanor Meredith, if it's a girl.

                          LIBBY
Eleanor? Why not Elizabeth? Or Libby?

LIBBY laughs at her own joke and everyone else joins in. MARIA cries out and bears down.
The baby finally slides out. The doctor passes it off to LIBBY.

                          DOCTOR
Eleanor it is, Maria.

                          MARIA
It's a girl? Is she all right?

                          LIBBY
                (as she wipes off the tiny baby)
Ten finger, ten toes.

MARIA cries out again and bears down again, just as the baby cries.

                          ELEANOR
What's happening, doctor?

                          DOCTOR
She should be passing the placenta now.
                              (looks)
Oh my god.

                          MARIA
Oh my god, what?!

                          DOCTOR
There's another one coming.

ELEANOR smiles excitedly at MARIA. LIBBY hands the swaddled baby girl to ELEANOR, who
takes her somewhat awkwardly, then begins to cuddle and talk to the baby, showing her to
MARIA. LIBBY readies new sheets for the second baby, smiling, fighting tears, as she takes it
from the doctor.

                          LIBBY
This one's Ben Junior.

As she swaddles the baby, LIBBY tries to dry her own tears.

EXT PAYNE PORCH AFTERNOON
BEN and MARIA, each holding a baby--the girl in pink, the boy in blue, swing in the loveseat.
NASH stands on a porch step near ELEANOR, who, although she's dressed in mourning, is
leaning against the railing admiring the babies.

                                ELEANOR
I still wish I could have a baby.

                                  BEN
You're young yet. I'm sure you'll remarry. Right, Nash?

                                 NASH
Yes, I'm sure when the right man comes along, Eleanor, you'll be ready to marry again.

                                ELEANOR
I'll never find another man like John.

                                 NASH
I know I'm a poor substitute for John, but would you consider going to the dance next
Saturday with me?

                                 MARIA
Yes, Eleanor. You haven't gotten out at all in the last three months. You need to start
living again.

                                ELEANOR
It was nice of the Army to agree to put me up for six months, wasn't it?

                                 NASH
They'd keep you longer, if you wanted to stay.
                         (moves up to sit next to her)
Will you just agree to go to the dance with me? Please?

                            MARIA AND BEN
                               (together)
Go. Have fun.

Everyone laughs. ELEANOR throws up her hands in defeat and nods her head. The babies
begin to cry.

INT OFFICERS BALLROOM EVENING
The military band plays as officers and their wives or dates dance. The room is decorated with
regimental regalia. A refreshment table sits at one end. It is covered with various finger foods
and a glass punch bowl with several glass cups.

NASH is in his dress uniform as he escorts ELEANOR, who is wearing a yellow dress, into the
room. He motions toward the dancers, and, after a few greetings, they join the dancers.
Dancers whirl past the refreshment table--with each sweep more food disappears. When there
is little food left, we return our focus on ELEANOR and NASH, who finish dancing and applaud
the band along with the few other couples remaining. ELEANOR fans herself and motions
toward the door. They step out on the veranda.

EXT VERANDA NIGHT
A couple of officers, who are smoking, are grouped together near the door. One couple stands
next to the rail a little way down. ELEANOR leads NASH further down where they lean on the
railing, looking out over the parade grounds.

                              NASH
I'm glad you came.

                            ELEANOR
So am I.

                              NASH
I think you're wonderful.

                            ELEANOR
You find me full of wonder?

                              NASH
I wonder how long it'll be before you let me kiss you.

                            ELEANOR
You don't want to kiss me.

                              NASH
Why don't I?

                            ELEANOR
It's a long story and I'm afraid you wouldn't understand. Let's walk, shall we?

ELEANOR leads NASH down the stairs and onto the parade grounds.

EXT   PARADE GROUNDS   NIGHT
ELEANOR heads for the row of cannons, which sit at one end of the field. She stops and leans
against the wheel of the third one, looking at the stars.

                            ELEANOR
Tell me, Capt. Nash, what do you see for the future?

                              NASH
Our future? Or that of our country?

                            ELEANOR
Our world.

                              NASH
That's a pretty big place.

                            ELEANOR
Makes you feel small, doesn't it?

                              NASH
Not when I'm next to you.

                            ELEANOR
                            (laughing)
You have a romantic response for everything, don't you?

                              NASH
Especially to you.

                              ELEANOR
I'm really flattered, Ora, I really am, but...I'm not the kind of woman you think I am.

                                NASH
What kind of woman is that?

                              ELEANOR
You don't want to know.

                                NASH
I wish you'd quit telling me I don't want to know something, dammit. I have a mind of
my own. Eyes and ears, too, for that matter.
                              (pauses)
And I know who you are.

                              ELEANOR
                          (paying attention)
You do? Who am I, then?

                                NASH
You're the future Mrs. Nash.

                              ELEANOR
                           (exasperated)
Really? Who made you lord and master over my fate?

                                NASH
John.

ELEANOR looks puzzled and angry. She starts to speak when NASH interrupts her.

                                NASH
He and I were more than friends. Much more.

                              ELEANOR
What do you mean? Much more?

                                NASH
                          (uncomfortable)
In the field, we were to each other what you two were to each other here.

                              ELEANOR
                          (fierce whisper)
He slept with you?

                                NASH
In every sense of the word.

                              ELEANOR
How? Why?

NASH

Military men often share blankets--for warmth, usually. Sometimes it becomes more. We...we had more.

ELEANOR

How long...Why didn't he ever tell me?

NASH

He wasn't sure how much of a woman you had become. He didn't know how you'd take it.

ELEANOR

Son of a bitch. The little.... Cheating on me.

ELEANOR, in her anger, starts to walk away. NASH quickly follows.

NASH

He always spoke highly of you. He never wanted to hurt you.

NASH reaches out and stops ELEANOR.

NASH (CONT)

I wouldn't have told you now, but...

ELEANOR

But what?

NASH

I wanted you to know what I am because...

ELEANOR

Because...?

NASH

I've loved you since I first saw you. I'd be honored if you'd be my...wife.

ELEANOR looks up at the stars.

INT FORT CHAPEL DAY
Dressed in her best white dress, ELEANOR and NASH exchange vows. MARIA and BEN, holding their babies, sit in the pews. LIBBY and the other officers' wives sit on the bride's side. Officers sit on the groom's. Pushing back her small veil, NASH softly kisses ELEANOR, and they walk down the aisle as friends congratulate them along the way. NEISMAN sits in the corner of the chapel.

INT NASH BEDROOM NIGHT
ELEANOR, still in her wedding dress, sits at a small desk in front of the window, writing in her diary. NASH comes in and stands behind her, putting his hands on her shoulders, then rubs her neck. She stops writing and stands, facing him. They undress each other slowly, then climb into bed together. NASH reaches up and turns down the lamp.

RETURN TO OPENING FRAME
INT   UNDERTAKER'S WORKROOM   MORNING
The undertaker sits, eating his lunch. ELEANOR's corpse lies covered by a sheet on a long table in the center of the room. The undertaker wipes his mouth and stands when two older men, the HEAD PHYSICIAN for the military hospital and the fort's CHAPLAIN, enter the room.

                         CHAPLAIN
          Is there something wrong with Mrs. Nash's body, sergeant?

                         UNDERTAKER
          Yes, sir, there is.

                         DOCTOR
          What is it, man, we haven't got all day. I've other flu victims to attend to who are still
          alive.

                         UNDERTAKER
          All I need to know, sirs, is what to do about this.

The UNDERTAKER sweeps back the sheet. Both men register shock with the CHAPLAIN looking to the doctor for reassurance of what he sees.

                         DOCTOR
          I assume Captain Nash knows about this.

                         CHAPLAIN
          It's most likely he does.

                         DOCTOR
          Does anyone else know?

                         UNDERTAKER
          As far as I know, just me.

                         CHAPLAIN
          It's a pity. Capt. Nash is due for promotion soon, too.

                         DOCTOR
                    (addressing chaplain)
          You know how news of this would make the Army look, don't you?

                         CHAPLAIN
          Of course, but...

                         DOCTOR
          No buts. Word of this isn't to go beyond this room. Do I make myself clear, reverend?

                         CHAPLAIN
          Yes, sir.

                         DOCTOR
          Sergeant?

UNDERTAKER
Yes, sir. Will you sign the certificate of death?

                      DOCTOR
Of course.
                       (signs)
Word has been sent to Nash?

                    UNDERTAKER
Not yet, sir. He's in Oklahoma Territory. A wire will be sent directly.

                      DOCTOR
Fine. Then stop over at the Nash quarters and see if she kept a diary or journal, just in
case. If you find one, burn it. Reverend, see to the funeral arrangements, will you?
                   (as he's leaving)
Make it a nice ceremony. He was a good woman.

AS END CREDITS ROLL

INT NASH BEDROOM AFTERNOON
The UNDERTAKER searches the bedroom, rifling through drawers, searching under the bed,
groping pillows, but finds nothing. The camera sees: a Chinese painting of a man with an
erection groping a woman. Behind the picture is a wooden door. Behind the door is a cubby
hole. In the cubby hole is ELEANOR's JOURNAL, which sits partially over the certificate of
marriage.

TO BLACK

Basic Math

Sharon Scholl

At first it's all addition –
growing a body up and out,
a twelve year stint at adding brains.

The rest piles on in swift succession:
job training, career, the first apartment,
before you know it, spouse and kids.

At middle age the balance sheet
swells and shrinks with births and deaths,
economic crash and boom

until the years signal reverse.
The rest of life is all subtraction –
the empty nest, retirement home,

blank days filled with minuses.
In old age we're doomed to play
that childhood game of take away.

Juvenile Blue Heron Stops by the Ventura, California Splashpad

Gerald Uyeno

Ode to a Sock

Karyn M. Bruce

For Anna Grace

We all have the same problem
when we reach inside the dresser drawer
and pull out. one. sock.
Then we rifle through the drawer
in search of the other. If not there,
do we wear the one sock? It looks like
we should. After all, it was waiting
inside the darkness we created for it.
Waiting. Did it know its other was missing?
Did it hide it? Did it toss its other half
behind the darkness? Did it want to be just one?

I don't match up to my mother, my father.
What were my siblings like? The ones
who died in the womb? Did we share the same
anything? I've spent my whole life
talking to myself about myself. Trying to wiggle
my way around my darkened boundaries. I didn't
work in a factory or wear house-dresses or pin-curls
in my hair. I tried not to flip around like one sock in the
middle of a dryer or dangle from a Mid-Western clothesline.
One. Sock. Twisting in the warm, spring winds hoping a starling
would not crap all over it flying by.

My granddaughter is delighted to wear mis-matched socks,
so when one pair is reduced to one. sock. she keeps it,
wears the odd sock with another odd sock.
Her drawer is full of purples, reds, stripes, and squiggly. odd. socks.
She thinks stores should sell them that way on purpose so
no. one. is looking for the other. one. It's fun, she says. I can wear more colors!
Ode to a Sock! It's glorious to be. One.

Venus' Looking Glass

Karen Colstrom

![photograph of a purple wildflower in a green field]

I don't want to die, I've got a test next

Gale Acuff

week and homework every day and who will
feed the dog and cat, my folks won't want to
but I want to visit the Afterlife
and that's the only way, I guess, croaking
that is, and then see Heaven and/or Hell
after I meet God and Jesus and all
the stuff lying for me and I just wish
that I could be dead for a little while
then come back to life--say *resurrection*,
but I'm no Son of God--then take up where
I left off although never wondering
and almost finished with my math homework,
long division it is and tough enough
to be divine. And I *do* mean divine.

Watcher

Jennifer Weigel

![Watcher illustration]

Octobers Yet to Come

Steve Brisendine

I should not read old ghost stories
on overcast autumn afternoons;

They make me wonder what sort
     of phantom I might become.

If we do sleepwalk, stirring in some
     dream of the Resurrection,

let me rise through chill free soil
and dry buffalo grass, slide between
brittle cottonwood leaves without
so much as a stray crackle and hitch
     a ride on the southwest wind.

Let me walk streets from Clay Avenue
to State Line Road, familiar grids and
diagonals leading both nowhere and to
     various familiar somewheres.

I do not aim to confront, to terrify,
to deliver dire warnings from Sheol;
let me be glimpsed sidelong, if at all,
     and only from behind.

Better still, if I have final say in the
manner of my manifestation, let me
be a whiff of pipe smoke, a scuff of
boots on asphalt, a breeze-whisper
     of frogsplash and banjo jazz.

Strawman

Jennifer Weigel

Unmoored

Franziska Roesner

I don't believe in prayer but
I wish I did. I wish I had

understood that my parents, too,
would get older, that my father's

limbs would stop responding
well, a kink in the neural hose

slowing water to a dribble,
that my mother's face would slowly

fold in upon itself like a
wet newspaper, that they

would watch for signs of their own
unmooring, that they

wouldn't mention any of this
to me.

Frozen

Jennifer Weigel

Territorial

Franziska Roesner

It rains so much this spring that
even the houses start growing,
sprouting windows where there had
been siding, bulbs bursting
into new rooms, carpeted as though with
pollen, spiral staircases wrapping
like vines and breaking
through attics, shingles hurrying,
fern-like, to fill in the gaps.
Monstrous and beautiful like
a strangely bulbed strawberry, like
a blackberry branch reaching, rooting
overnight in the next yard over.
When the rains pass, do we weed it?
Do we leave? Or can we stay?

Sweet Summer

Karen Colstrom

Contributors' Notes

Producers and production companies interested in performing any of the plays or screenplays should first contact the writer through the contact information listed here. If they do not provide a method of contacting them there, please contact Choeofpleirn Press through choeofpleirnpress@gmail.com.

Gale Acuff has had hundreds of poems published in a dozen countries and has authored three books of poetry. His poems have appeared in *Ascent, Reed, Arkansas Review, Poem, Slant, Aethlon, Florida Review, South Carolina Review, Carolina Quarterly, Roanoke Review, Danse Macabre, Ohio Journal, Sou'wester, South Dakota Review, North Dakota Quarterly, New Texas, Midwest Quarterly, Poetry Midwest, Adirondack Review, Worcester Review, Adirondack Review, Connecticut River Review, Delmarva Review, Maryland Poetry Review, Maryland Literary Review, George Washington Review, Pennsylvania Literary Journal, Ann Arbor Review, Plainsongs, Chiron Review, George Washington Review, McNeese Review, Weber, War, Literature & the Arts, Poet Lore, Able Muse, The Font, Fine Lines, Teach.Write., Oracle, Hamilton Stone Review, Sequential Art Narrative in Education, Cardiff Review, Tokyo Review, Indian Review, Muse India, Bombay Review, Westerly*, and many other journals. Gale has taught tertiary English courses in the US, PR China, and Palestine.

Brian C. Billings is a professor of drama and English at Texas A&M University-Texarkana and the editor-in-chief for *Aquila Review*, the university's literary journal. In addition to managing TAMU-T's drama program, he teaches courses in drama, creative writing, and children's literature. His work has appeared in such journals as *Antietam Review, Ancient Paths, Argestes, Backstreet Quarterly, Confrontation, Evening Street Review, Poems and Plays*, and *Rushing Thru the Dark*. Publishers for his scripts include Eldridge Publishing and Heuer Publishing. For more information about his work, please contact him at brianbillings625@gmail.com.

Steve Brisendine lives, works and remains unbeaten against *The New York Times* crossword in Mission, Kansas. He is the author of five collections of poetry, most recently *full of old books and silence* (Alien Buddha Press, 2024) and *Beyond the Wall Cloud of Sleep* (Spartan Press, 2024). His work has appeared in *Modern Haiku, I-70 Review, Flint Hills Review* and other publications and compilations. He has no degrees, one tattoo and a deep and unironic fondness for strip-mall Chinese restaurants. In his spare time, he tries to make himself seem far more interesting than he actually is.

Karyn M. Bruce is a poet who lives in Miami, Florida. She holds a BFA in Creative Writing from Bowling Green State University, Ohio, and two degrees from Barry University, FL: an MFA in Literature and an Ed.S. in Education. Although retired from teaching middle school English and her professorship in Freshman English at Johnson & Wales University, she is currently teaching at the Alternative Education Academy in Miami, FL. to students with disabilities. She has published two books of poetry: *I Will Write Loudly So You Can Hear Me* (2018) and *Compline* (2023). Her email address is ikarynbruce@gmail.com. She lives with her husband, Steven, and two cocker spaniels, Lucie Marie and Lillie Joel.

David Capps is a philosophy professor and writer living in New Haven, Connecticut. He is the author of six chapbooks: *Poems from the First Voyage* (The Nasiona Press, 2019), *A Non-Grecian Non-Urn* (Yavanika Press, 2019), *Colossi* (Kelsay Books, 2020), *On the Great Duration of Life* (Schism Neuronics, 2023), *Wheatfield with a Reaper* (Akinoga Press, forthcoming), and *Fever in Bodrum* (Bottlecap Press, forthcoming). His latest lyric essay is featured in *Midnight Chem*.

Natalie Castagnola studied English Education and loves to practice her skills in writing. She particularly enjoys writing about navigating her life after growing up in an orthodox religion. She enjoys traveling and is currently living/traveling in Europe, which also plays a significant role in her writing. Her hobbies include reading, going for walks, and quality time with loved ones. Her work has been published at *Seedlings Poets,* and you can follow her on Instagram at natcastag. You can also follow her personal blog callmebymynewnameblog.com.

Loralee Clark is a writer who grew up learning a love for nature and her place in it, in Maine. She resides in Virginia now as a writer and artist, with two awesome kids and a loving husband. Her Instagram is @make13experiment. She writes poetry and non-fiction. Myth is her love language. My publication credentials include the upcoming *The Archivist: An Anthology for Creative Journaling Artists*, *The Pagan's Muse: Words of Ritual, Invocation, and Inspiration*, Ed. Jane Raeburn, as well as the poetry journals *The Taborian*, *Superpresent*, *Thimble Literary Magazine*, *Impossible Task*, *Studio One*, *Cannon's Mouth*, *Big Windows Review*, *Broadkill Review*, *Literary Mama*, *The Binnacle*, and *Penwood Review*.

Karen Colstrom is a native-born Kansan who grew up on the farm. She has a background in art, graduating from Emporia State University. Karen taught a children's program for 20 years, sharing her love of art. Her current passion is photography on the family farm. Karen's photography is inspired by the beauty of nature. She has a website: prairiedesignphotography.com.

James P. Cooper, a Pushcart nominee, has had poems appear in *Apple Valley Review*, *Evening Street Review*, *Slant*, *Stone Poetry Quarterly*, and other journals. His chapbook, *Listening for Low Tide*, was awarded an honorable mention in the chapbook category of the 2024 Eric Hoffer Book Award. He teaches college writing and lives in Leavenworth, Kansas with his wife and many cats.

John Delaney's publications include *Waypoints* (2017), a collection of place poems, *Twenty Questions* (2019*)*, a chapbook, *Delicate Arch* (2022), poems and photographs of national parks and monuments, and *Galápagos* (2023), a collaborative chapbook of his son Andrew's photographs and his poems. *Nile*, a chapbook of poems and photographs about Egypt, appeared in May 2024. He lives in Port Townsend, Washington.

Stephen Philip Druce is a poet and short story writer from Shrewsbury in the United Kingdom.

Glenn Falacienski lives in New Mexico and studies English at Colorado College. She worked as a political journalist for *Affinity Magazine* before getting published in *Cipher Magazine*; *YOGURT Culture Zine*; *Blue Marble Review*; *The Handy, Uncapped Pen*; and *HNDL Mag*, among others. Glenn's greatest talent is the ability to hula-hoop and read at the same time.

Frank William Finney is a poet from Massachusetts. A Joint winner of The Letter Review Prize for Poetry, his poems have been published by *Blue Unicorn, Drawn to the Light Press, Glacial Hills Review, Persephone Literary Magazine,* and elsewhere. His chapbook *The Folding of the Wings* was published in 2022 (FLP Books).

Andrew Graber is a self-taught artist who was born and raised in the northeast part of the United States. He currently calls the beautiful state of Nevada his home. Besides creating various forms of artwork, Andy also has strong interests in writing and music.

Paweł Grajnert is a writer and filmmaker working in Poland and the United States.

Susan Hansell <https://www.susan-hansell.net/> is a full voting member of the Dramatist Guild of America <https://www.dramatistsguild.com/members/susanhansell>. Her play *Letters to Jeff Bezos* began as a single monologue published in the 2022 edition of *Rushing Thru the Dark* and subsequently developed into a full-length play that will be presented as a rehearsed staged reading in September 2024 by the Topanga Actors Company. *Dear Jeff Bezos* is an excerpt from this new two-act play, which is listed, as are all of her plays, with the New Play Exchange <https://newplayexchange.org/users/5806/susan-hansell>.

Ruth J. Heflin did not predict Jesus would appear on the Benny Hinn show, but she did survive growing up in the buckle of the bible belt with the name "Ruth." She still lives there with two cats and a husband, practicing her scholarship to write *Pitiless Bronze: A Postpatriarchal Examination of Prepatriarchal Cultures*, which reexamines cultural myths and archeological finds from a gynocentric perspective, while also writing other things and spending most of her time editing for Choeofpleirn Press.

Duane L. Herrmann, internationally published, award-winning poet and historian, has work in print and on-line in *Midwest Quarterly, Little Balkans Review, Flint Hills Review, Manifest West, Inscape, Gonzo Press, Tiny Seed Literary Journal,* plus over one hundred other publications, over sixty anthologies, and a sci fi novel. His full-length collections of poetry include: *Prairies of Possibilities, Ichnographical: 173, Praise the King of Glory, No Known Address, Remnants of a Life, Family Plowing, Zephyrs of the Heart,* and *Into the Wind*. His poetry has received the Robert Hayden Poetry Fellowship, inclusion in *American Poets of the 1990s,* Map of Kansas Literature, Kansas Poets Trail, and others. This, despite an abusive childhood embellished by dyslexia, ADHD, cyclothymia, an anxiety disorder, and now, PTSD. He has carried baby kittens in his mouth, petted snakes, and held conversations with owls, but is careful not to anger them! He was surprised to find himself on a farm in Kansas and is still trying to make sense of that, but has grown fond of grass waving under wind, trees, and the enchantment of moonlight.

Elly Katz, at 27, verging towards a doctorate at Harvard went to a doctor for mundane procedure to stabilize her neck. Upon waking from anesthesia, she searched in vain for the right half of her body. Somehow, she survived what doctors surmised was unsurvivable: a brainstem stroke secondary to a physician's needle misplacement. Her path towards science, amongst other ambitions, came to a halt. As a devout writer, she feared that poetry, too, fell outside what was possible given her inert right fingers. However, in the wake of tragedy, she discovered the power of dictation and the bounty of metaphor.

Kenneth Kesner (肯内思) splits his time between the Caucasus and South East Asia. Some recent works are featured in: *Levitate Magazine, New Note Poetry, Poetry Pacific, October Hill Magazine* and *Wayne Literary Review.*

Craig Kirchner thinks of poetry as hobo art, loves storytelling and the aesthetics of the paper and pen. He has had two poems nominated for the Pushcart, and has a book of poetry, *Roomful of Navels.* After a writing hiatus he was recently published in *Decadent Review, Wild Violet, Last Leaves, Literary Heist, Cape Magazine, Chiron Review, Valiant Scribe, Unlikely Stories, Coneflower Cafe, Glacial Hills Review, Yellow Mama, The Argyle, Hamilton Stone Review, The Main Street Rag,* and several dozen other journals.

Carlee Klipsun is a disabled writer and artist from the Pacific Northwest now living in rural Georgia. She received her B.A. in Creative Writing from Western Washington University and her M.A. in Conflict Transformation and Social Justice at Queen's University Belfast. Her previous written work has been published in WWU's *Jeopardy Magazine* and the Confluence Project's *Voices of the River.* When not writing, Carlee spends her time volunteering for her tribe (the Chinook Indian Nation), making earrings, and herding cats.

Richard Lehan is a fiction writer and essayist living in Massachusetts. Most recently, his short story *Ambulatory* appeared in the Spring 2024 edition of *Coneflower Cafe* magazine; his flash fiction "State Forest," appeared in the 2024 edition of *Stolen Shoes Literary & Art Magazine*. *Conflagration* is his first play.

Amy Lerman was born and raise don Miami Beach,moved to the Midwest for many years, and now lives with her husband and very spoiled cats in the Arizona desert. She is residential English Faculty at Mesa Community College, and her poems have appeared in *Willawaw Journal, Stonecoast Review*, *Broad River Review*, *Radar Poetry*, *Rattle, Slippery Elm*, and other publications. Her poem, "Why Is It?" was the inaugural winner of the Art Young Memorial Award for Poetry.

Dave Malone is a poet and playwright who lives in the Missouri Ozarks. He spent his early childhood in Riley, Kansas, and later graduated from Olathe North High School. He holds degrees from Ottawa University and Indiana State University. A three-time Pushcart nominee, he is the author of eight collections of poetry, most recently *Bypass* (Kelsay Books, 2023). His work has been featured on NPR and appeared in *Midwest Review, San Pedro River Review,* and *Red Rock Review*. He offers a free monthly e-newsletter. More at *davemalone.net*.

Megan Munger is a Kansas poet and Pacific University MFA Candidate. She received her M.A. and B.S.Ed. in English from Pittsburg State University, where she received the James B.M. Schick *Midwest Quarterly* Graduate Studies Best Essay Award in 2021 and 2022. She currently resides in Junction City, KS, where she teaches English at Junction City High School. Her poetry has previously appeared in the *Of Our Own Accord* anthology by Flying Ketchup Press and online at *Kitchen Table Quarterly* and *The Coop: A Poetry Cooperative*.

Sherrie Pesta, PhD is a theatre educator and practitioner. Her previously published plays include: *Pencils, Paper, and Poison* with Heartland Plays (2019); *The Beach Umbrella* with Choeofpleirn Press (2021), a Susan Hansell Drama Prize winner; *Find a Penny with* Choeofpleirn Press (2022); and *The Hot House* with Nervous Ghost Press (2023). She recently enjoyed having a theatre-for-youth script, *The Mystery of the Missing Clauses*, produced by The Quannapowitt Players (2023).

Michael Riordan has taught in the U.S., Australia, Singapore, and China, where he was a professor of writing, western culture, and film. In Singapore, he co-founded Creative Action Now, a language school and consultancy. He has written several plays for schools and community theater; his nonfiction, short stories and poetry can be found in *Short Edition, Multiplicity, Glacial Hills Review, Consequence, Whimsical Poet, Spirituality & Health,* and elsewhere. He and his wife Mary, a speech-language pathologist, live in Arlington, Texas. Portfolio: www.clippings.me/wordsticks

Franziska (Franzi) Roesner holds a PhD in computer science and is a professor at the University of Washington in Seattle, teaching and researching computer security and privacy. She was a poet before she was a computer scientist, though, and she has returned to poetry in the last few years. She lives in Seattle with her husband, two daughters, and one remaining cat. You can find her website at https://www.franziroesner.com/poetry.

David Sapp, writer, artist, and professor, lives along the southern shore of Lake Erie in North America. A *Pushcart* nominee, he was awarded Ohio Arts Council Individual Excellence Grants for poetry and the visual arts. His poetry and prose appear widely in the United States, Canada, and the United Kingdom. His publications include articles in the *Journal of Creative Behavior*, chapbooks *Close to Home* and *Two Buddha*, a novel *Flying Over Erie,* and a book of poems and drawings titled *Drawing Nirvana*.

Cecil Sayre's poems have appeared in *Naugatuck River Review*, *Levitate*, *Valley Voices*, and *Two Hawks Quarterly*, along with many other literary journals.

Benjamin Schmitt is the Elgin Award-nominated author of four books, most recently *The Saints of Capitalism* and *Soundtrack to a Fleeting Masculinity*. His poems have appeared in *Sojourners,*

Antioch Review, The Good Men Project, Hobart, Columbia Review, Spillway, and elsewhere. A co-founder of Pacifica Writers' Workshop, he has also written articles for *The Seattle Times* and *At The Inkwell.* He lives in Seattle with his wife and children.

Sharon Scholl is a retired college teacher who convenes a poetry critique group and maintains a website of original music free for small, liberal churches. Her poetry chapbooks, *Seasons, Remains, Evensong,* are available via Amazon Books. Her poems are currently in *Third Wednesday* and *Epistemic Library.*

Daniel P. Stokes has published poetry widely in literary magazines in Ireland, Britain, the U.S.A, Canada and Asia, and has won several poetry prizes. He has written three stage plays which have been professionally produced in Dublin, London and at the Edinburgh Festival.

Gerald Uyeno makes his living as an engineer: writing science fiction and creating graphic images of the future. He also enjoys creating visual artwork with pencil, pen, or computer, and in the past several years, he has taken a keen interest in photography as an art form.

Jennifer Weigel is a multi-disciplinary mixed media conceptual artist. Weigel utilizes a wide range of media to convey her ideas, including assemblage, drawing, fibers, installation, jewelry, painting, performance, photography, sculpture, video and writing. Much of her work touches on themes of beauty, identity (especially gender identity), memory & forgetting, an institutional critique. Weigel's art has been exhibited nationally in all 50 states and has won numerous awards.

Born in Pennsylvania and educated in New York and Wisconsin, **Allison Whittenberg** is an award-winning novelist and playwright. Her poetry has appeared in *Columbia Review, Feminist Studies, J Journal,* and *New Orleans Review.* Whittenberg is a six-time Pushcart Prize nominee. *Driving with a Poetic License* and *They Were Horrible Cooks* are her collections of poetry. "Ride the Peter Pan" was the first short story featured in the collection *Carnival of Reality* (2022).

McKenna Wilds is a poet and storyteller whose writing often delves into themes of womanhood, folklore, friendship, and family. She lives in Colorado with her husband and goldendoodle. Her work can be found in *Marathon Literary Review.* Connect with her on Instagram as @mckenna.wilds.

Diane Zoeller is a poet residing on Long Island in New York. Diane's poetry reflects a determination to seek out life's joys especially while overcoming sorrow. Her poems capture moments in her life and reflect the lives of family members who have helped to shape her world view. Diane has recently retired from a long career in education, giving her the luxury of writing full-time. When she is not writing, Diane spends her time reading, volunteering, and gushing over her grandchildren.

Ads

JENNIFER WEIGEL
Fine Art
Home
Drawings
Paintings
Photography
Jewelry
Bio

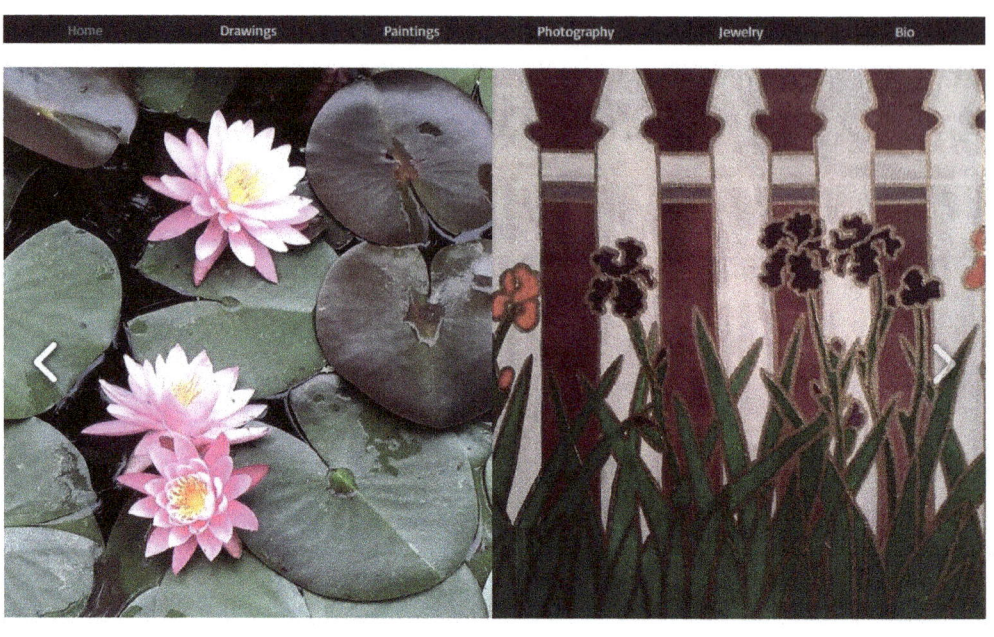

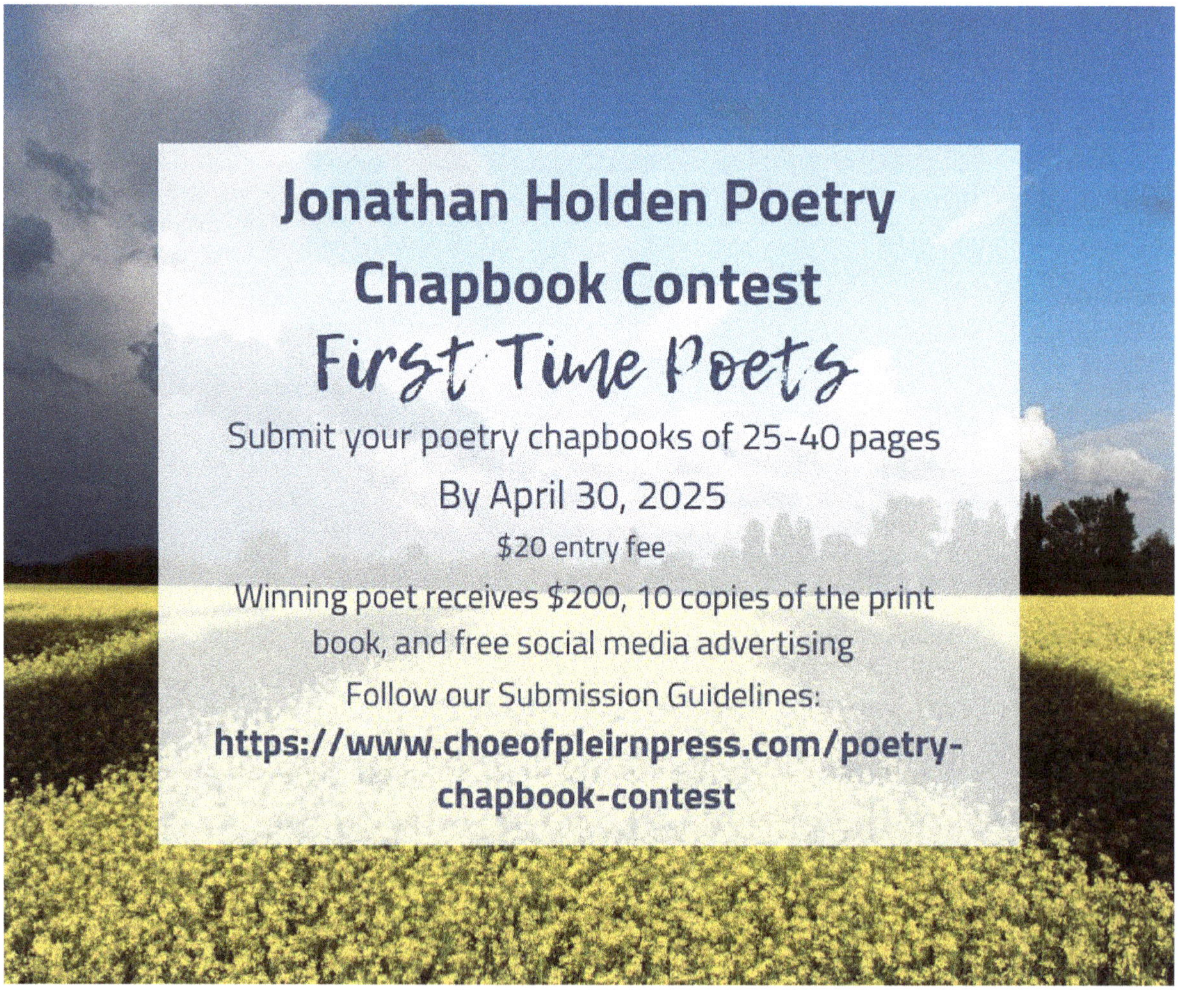
Jonathan Holden Poetry
Chapbook Contest
First Time Poets
Submit your poetry chapbooks of 25-40 pages
By April 30, 2025
$20 entry fee
Winning poet receives $200, 10 copies of the print book, and free social media advertising
Follow our Submission Guidelines:
https://www.choeofpleirnpress.com/poetry-chapbook-contest

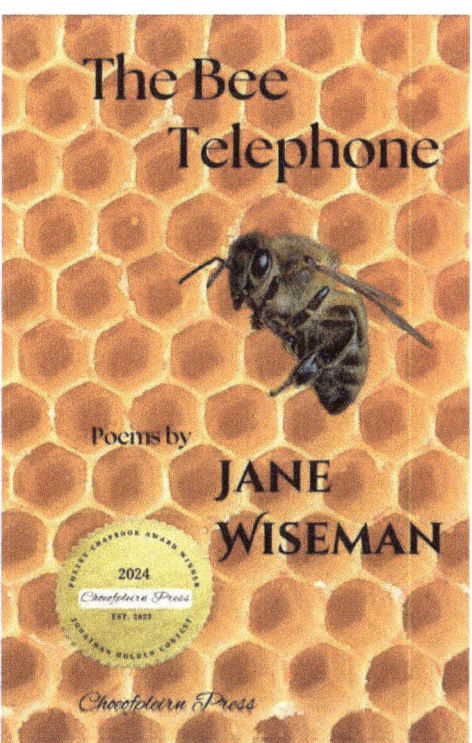

2024 Winner
Jonathan Holden Poetry Chapbook Contest

Hosted by
Choeofpleirn Press

Imagine picking up a phone and hearing an alien voice or pressing our noses against glass to watch aliens work.

Jane Wiseman allows us to tune in to the sights and sounds of our universe, even though they may seem as alien as listening to *The Bee Telephone*.

1st Finalist
2024
Jonathan Holden
Poetry Chapbook Contest

Hosted by

Choeofpleirn Press

These poems are about awe, about how the simplest moments of our lives are the most important—sharing stories with family in the car or on the boat, that first kiss with a future spouse "for no reason" (which he knows is actually the best reason). Most people don't realize until much later how important these quiet moments, these "bright whispers" are, but what makes Shrum's work so extraordinary is that he understands their reverence as he lives them.

Melissa Fite Johnson,
author of *Midlife Abecedarian* and *Green*.

2nd Finalist

Jonathan Holden Poetry Chapbook Contest 2024

How do we shake the detritus from our memories? A geographic transplant, Rochelle Germond washes clean those memories she rediscovers before leaving those excavations behind to discover not only what can frighten her but also what gives meaning to this new location where "the wishbone we snap breaks evenly in half, / a sure sign that we will both receive our pleas."

James P. Cooper

Author of *Listening for Low Tide*
Honorable Mention for the Eric Hoffer Book Award

Tracy Robert's mother in a photo used on a brochure and banner for LACMA's Gilbert Adrian exhibition. She was a beautiful, complicated, difficult woman, and it was hard to be her daughter. *Angora Panties: The Afterthoughts of Loss* is about Robert making peace with her mother's memory, among other things.

Listening for Low Tide

Available at Amazon and
Choeofpleirn Press

Too much happens at ground level:
the kids selling candy or delivering
newspapers shortcut through the yard,
the neighbors' dogs blare their alarms
in unison, and teens, shielded by the heartbeat
of their music, speed down the street.

Two stories above the ground.
I welcome the afternoon sunlight
as it stretches across the rug,
my cat moving with it. From the opposite
window, the shadows cast by trees
overspread the ground, the sunlight only
hitting the treetops. Sound waves lap
against the building, the tide at its lowest
each night when the owl in the park
starts to hoot its presence.

Honorable Mention for the Eric Hoffer Book Award 2024

Choeofpleirn Press

A Kansas private
literary press

www.choeofpleirnpress.com

A 501(3)(c) company

Using the scientific process, Heflin re-examines ancient artifacts and myths from the ancient world to demonstrate how women's ties to the cosmos were honored and revered. From being able to bleed, but not die, for 3-5 days, to having menstrual cycles in sync with the moon-- ancient women exercised Feminine Power, a power so fierce that modern patriarchists denigrate trans women and drag queens who have embraced it.

Learn why patriarchists want us to believe that patriarchies have always existed, when, in fact, they only arose after 2400 BCE, when Egyptians determined that males actually play a role in procreation.

The evidence is written for both lay and scholarly readers, so that everyone can learn the real truth.

Print copies are available wherever you buy books. The digital copy can be purchased through Choeofpleirn Press.

PITILESS BRONZE

A Postpatriarchal Examination of Prepatriarchal Cultures

Ruth J. Heflin, PhD

Choeofpleirn Press

www.choeofpleirnpress.com
choeofpleirnpress@gmail.com

Copyright 2024

www.ingramcontent.com/pod-product-compliance
Lightning Source LLC
Chambersburg PA
CBHW051851140626
46547CB00034BA/3011